TRAVEL BECOMES US

by

LUCILLE HINTZE

authorHOUSE®

AuthorHouse™
1663 Liberty Drive
Bloomington, IN 47403
www.authorhouse.com
Phone: 1-800-839-8640

Published by AuthorHouse 10/16/2014

ISBN: 978-1-4184-6768-5 (sc)
ISBN: 978-1-4685-1323-3 (e)

Library of Congress Control Number: 2004093773

DEDICATION

TO TRAVELERS AND TO THOSE
WHO WRITE THE
TRAVEL BOOKS THAT MAKE
THEIR DREAMS COME TRUE

Table of Contents

CHAPTER I
Packing Chaos...1
CHAPTER II
"Flying High"..7
CHAPTER III
Across the Water to Lisbon...11
CHAPTER IV
The Sophistication and Grandeur of Spain 17
CHAPTER V
Israel - June 23rd to July 26th..35
SECTION I
Off to Galilee! 51
SECTION II
The Holy City 63
SECTION III
Modern Memories...77
SECTION IV
Back To The Franciscan Sisters 81
CHAPTER VI
The Glory of Athens..97
CHAPTER VII
The Eternal City of Rome 103
CHAPTER VIII
More Italian Adventures 115
CHAPTER IX
Alpine Meadows and Waterfalls 127
CHAPTER X
Rain, Dark Glasses at Midnight and Venice 141

CHAPTER XI
Back to Hill Country 145
CHAPTER XII
Adventures in Germany 151
CHAPTER XIII
Onward to Paris..159
CHAPTER XIV
Clean Air, Healthy Appetites and Sparkling Waters 165
CHAPTER XV
Windmills, Dikes, and Belgian Hospitality 175
CHAPTER XVI
Honest Scotsmen and Clan Tartans............................181
CHAPTER XVII
London Town 185
CHAPTER XVIII
Homeward Bound 189
OUR ITINERARY 191

CHAPTER I
PACKING CHAOS

Why were two Catholic Sisters frantically packing at the midnight hour? While all the good sisters in their convent home were peacefully sleeping the sleep of the just? The reason? We were packing for a fabulous trip to the HOLY LAND!

We, Sister Lorraine and I, Sister Lucille, had just received our doctorates in Scripture from San Francisco Theological! The trip was a graduation gift from our parents. They, being practical, thought that if we were to teach about the Bible, we ought to have firsthand knowledge about the HOLY LAND, not just mere book learning. This was a gift of realizing in actuality what we had only read about before in books. We now could walk where Jesus had trod and see the same countryside. We thought to reconstruct the events of His life from birth to Resurrection and then follow the missionary journeys of the Apostles in spreading the Good News. This was the carrot held out in front of us as we had studied over the passage of the past six years. A rather formidable task as, back in the 70s, we did not receive time off to pursue our degrees. We had to carry on our regular work as principals in our schools of religion during the school year, and then take our scripture and theology courses in the summer. But, of course, the final hurdle to surmount was the writing of our dissertations. Then came the agony of waiting to see if our papers would be accepted. Those tensions and struggles are a story unto themselves and are only mentioned here because this trip of ours was to be the climax of those years of study.

When we realized that our dream trip could be or WOULD BE in the summer of our graduation, we started to plan during any free time we could find: on the way to work, lunch breaks, late evenings. Our parents had offered $1,500 for our travel expenses. How far could we stretch this amount?

First, we needed to figure out how long we could be away without causing havoc in the reopening of our schools in the Fall. Sister Lorraine and I were immersed in the day-to-day struggle of the ordinary business of running our two Schools of Religion. Plus now we were trying both to close for the summer and to plan ahead for reopening in the Fall. Could we, as principals, foresee all eventualities, opening letters to parents and students, schedules for classes, etc., so that the necessary work for pre-opening could successfully begin in the Fall without our being there physically to supervise? Could we, in planning, turn the clock forward and backward enough to realize how to successfully extend our trip into late August or even just before opening day in September? This was our ambitious goal. Was this possible? Should we risk it? We did have a willing staff if we had it all organized.

Now if we had all these months, how much could we see and do during this long interval of time? We had thought to start from Bethlehem, the birth place of Jesus, next to retrace the Holy Family's flight into Egypt, and then back to Nazareth. Not possible! Modern political events and economic considerations had a way of intervening into one's plans. It was impossible to "fly into Egypt" from Israel in the year 1977. Of course we could have flown to Egypt first, but that didn't prove either economical or time-wise feasible. So we planned and replanned how to get the most mileage and the most stopovers covered. Finally the pieces fell into place and we had our itinerary. The Holy Land was our first and main concern. But that didn't prevent us from thinking how we could stretch out our trip to include Greece and Europe! How Christianity spread into other countries was also important to us. So we stole away precious time to transfer our dreams into reality. I would say, "I would like to see..." and Lorraine would answer "Let's." Then she would say, "I'd like to visit..." and I would reply, "We'll add it in..." When we had finished our itinerary, the design of our trip resembled a gigantic cloverleaf. So we never had to backtrack. We were very determined to see everything possible in our allotted time, as we were positive that "we would never pass this way again!"

Ruth, our travel agent, was alternately concerned and exhilarated over our itinerary. "Never would there be such a trip! The Holy Land is not too complicated. But Europe is another matter!" she exclaimed. "I fear the scheduling is much too complicated for two such inexperienced novices at travel. You will miss your trains and lose your way. Five minutes to find another train in a strange station? Impossible!" But nevertheless she patiently taught me to read Cook's Timetable for Trains. Lorraine and I had divided our duties. I was to schedule and find the right track and train coach. She would see to the maneuvering of our luggage (no light or easy task, as it turned out). Then Ruth gave us a book that was to become our constant faithful companion, Arthur Frommer's Touring Europe on $5 and $10 a day. At the moment we didn't realize what a vital treasure had been placed into our hands!

Meanwhile, Lorraine consulted the climate charts for the various countries and discovered the temperatures ranged from the extremes of 125 in the desert of Israel to 22 below in the ice caverns of the Jungfrau, plus everything in between! Cool cottons and warmer polyesters; what about shoes? Oh, so many questions to be answered. And we did get answers and advice from those who had "gone before." Some times, however, the opinions were conflicting! We became confused.

AT LAST THE FINAL WEEKEND ARRIVED!!!!

We excitedly graduated with our class after years of Scripture Study on that very special Friday. Saturday we spent with our families. Sunday we thought to pack for our trip, but the Sisters in our convent decided it was much more important to have a Celebration for us. We couldn't sneak away. We were the guests of honor! Worse luck! At last, the conversations dwindled down to the last goodbyes and our thanks for the Sisters' good wishes. We, then, dashed madly upstairs. This was our first chance to pack! By this time, however, it was hovering close to the midnight hour on the 12th of June. And with or without us, our plane was scheduled to leave early the next morning on Monday, the 13th!!

Friends, take a word of advice from two now-seasoned travelers. Don't attempt to fill your suitcases for a three-month trip, tiptoeing around in the dead of night immediately after the thrill and exhaustion of a struggle to obtain your degree! Of course, the inevitable happened; we lost track of what we were packing. Lorraine was ransacking our rooms to bring out everything she thought we might need. My job was to pack. Our parents, bless their hearts, had given us two Lark suitcases. One suitcase apiece! First, I packed the large suitcase to the top and running over; then the smaller one, but still the stuff kept coming! Lorraine kept rushing from our rooms bringing out more and more clothes, medicines, paper products, travel gifts from our friends, etc. I guess neither of us thought THAT there just might be a drug store outside of the U.S.A.!

Lorraine's cousin had also given her a very fashionable designer bag as a gift for graduation. The type a sophisticated woman would carry lightly over her shoulder. Lorraine never had the chance to act out that role, for I crammed her poor bag full to the bursting point! Yet there was still a pile of odds and ends left over that just couldn't be fitted in anywhere. But who would stay home because of this? Not us! I dashed to the kitchen and returning, dumped this overflow into two large shopping bags. Meanwhile, Lorraine practiced how to flip open the luggage cart. She became a master at this after several agonizing tries. Then the clock tolled 3 a.m.!

A scant three hours of sleep and we were whisked to the San Francisco airport before sunup. Here a stern airline official frowned a "no" to our two bulging shopping bags! This absolutely wouldn't do! How strange that we were traveling with only a suitcase apiece! Two might have been better. However, a much kinder agent took pity on us and produced a rectangular box with a cardboard handle into which everything from the bags was tightly jammed. For the moment, the problem was solved. But don't fool yourself; this box was only resting quietly for the moment. In reality, it was "out to get us," two unwary novice travelers. But more about that later.

Our flight was called. Our goodbyes were said. Our "Great Adventure" had begun-- Monday, June 13, 1977.

TRAVELERS SETTING FORTH
WITH THEIR SUITCASES BULGING.
WAS SO MUCH REALLY NEEDED?

LUCILLE HINTZE

CHAPTER II
"FLYING HIGH"

As we walked with our luggage toward the waiting TWA plane, two stewardesses fell into step with us. Exchanging travel information, we found to our delight that they were part of the crew on our flight from San Francisco to New York. Their thoughtfulness on the trip was a blessing, for the two of us were flying higher than even the plane. Too much had been crowded into these last few days. Our minds were running wildly in an attempt to catch up to our physical bodies flying in an airplane over the U.S. Continent. We tried to convince ourselves that we no longer had any pressing loose ends. Relax! We told ourselves. Don't worry! Can't do anything about it now. Just sit back in your seats. Look out the window. Enjoy the scenery. So we tried to distract our minds from our yesterdays and into the present. We noted the steep climb over the Sierra Nevada Mountains. We scanned the arid section of land below us in Nevada and Utah. We saw the broad expanse of the Great Salt Lake glistening below us and Salt Lake City, itself, nestling smack up against the towering Rockies. Far below the plane, like chilly fingers, long white ribbons of snow were flung against the steep sides of the Rockies. We shivered as we looked down. Suppose we crashed there and had to climb out? We checked the TWA map. Our route was central-south over Colorado and a corner of Wyoming near Cheyenne. We glued ourselves to the window.

Then the stewardess was bending over us asking us what we would like to eat. The reality of meal time recalled us to the needs of our hungry bodies. Dinner was served: Chicken

Breast Coconut for Sister Lorraine, Hungarian Beef Goulash for Sister Lucille. Maybe it was just our nervous tummies, but the food definitely did not taste that good to us, although the service was excellent.

Fortunately the co-pilot alerted us from time to time as to which section of our vast country we were flying over. Our fears abated slowly. We wondered about great circular plots resembling huge pies on the flatlands of Nebraska. Strange! Sometimes the green circles would have brown wedges in them. We never did fathom the mystery. Also there were faint horizontal markings. Could these be rows upon rows of corn?

Then a cloud blanket formed beneath us, blotting out the rest of the terrain until we were well over Pennsylvania coming into New York. If we couldn't watch the ground, TWA was prompt to entertain their passengers with a movie. So for an hour and a half, we laughed and laughed at the comic situations that developed when a mother and a daughter found themselves switched into each other's bodies for a day. It was Walt Disney's "Frantic Friday." It's not so easy to walk in another's shoes, even for one day. We had enough problems ourselves just trying to change into relaxing tourists.

Suddenly we were circling the tall skyscrapers of New York and gliding into J.F. Kennedy Airport. It was 7 p.m. E.S.T., but 4 p.m. our time. Gathering our "carry-ons," we walked briskly along in the terminal with all our luggage trundling merrily along after us.

We had arrived! First thing was to find a telephone and call our parents. Sister Lorraine tried to call her folks. They weren't home. I dialed. Neither was my Mom. What a letdown! Why weren't our parents home waiting for a call from their offspring? Weren't they the least bit worried about us? They knew we had never been outside the country before! Lorraine had never been out of California! What to do? Finally we telephoned Lois, our good friend. At least she was home! Lois promised to let our parents and the Sisters know that we had arrived safely in New York. A bitter solace for these two disappointed hopefuls at the telephone booth.

LUCILLE HINTZE

CHAPTER III
ACROSS THE WATER TO LISBON

The next leg of our journey was about to begin! Bravely, we strode across the enormous airport lobby toward our new boarding gate. But trouble was brewing. Our last minute "carry-on box" was about to collapse! We frantically tried to buy a luggage strap or at least some twine, but we found nothing useful. However, once again, a luggage attendant came to the rescue -- this time by band-aiding the box with tape from top to bottom. For the moment, the box seemed subdued, but mischief lurked maliciously beneath those innocent rolls of tape.

By 8:30 p.m. E.S.T., our transatlantic plane was rising gallantly into the air, with the lights of New York twinkling below.

How different from the Pacific side the Atlantic seacoast appeared. Flat marshy inlets, like our Sacramento Delta, flowed gently into the Atlantic's smoother coastal line. People's homes bordered the straight sandy beaches. We had just a short glimpse of this shoreline before the plane quickly headed out over the ocean. Then only blue waters were below us. Not enough variety there to distract us. Soon our forgotten bodies began to feel hunger pains. We looked around to see that the stewardess was already serving dinner. So we straightened up and took notice. This time, Short Ribs Jardiniere was served to Lorraine, and Barbecued Chicken Breast to Lucille. Everything tasted so so good for, fortunately, the butterflies in our stomachs had settled down to rest. On into the darkness we flew, and off went the lights in the plane.

Time for a tear-jerker movie "Islands in the Sea" by Ernest Hemingway. However, before it began the stewardess startled us all into sudden laughter by telling us to pull down the window shades so the daylight wouldn't bother us. The night was pitch black outside! But before the end of the movie, we secretly peeked out through the curtains to discover that the sky was reddening around the edges of massive black clouds that resembled bridges between castle battlements. Then the sun came bounding up... round, brilliant, red, and glorious.

Oh, the two of us did grow tired on the plane and we did try to sleep. But we really couldn't. All was so easy at the New York airport, but soon we would be landing in Portugal.

TWA flight 900 actually crossed the Atlantic in 12 hours depositing us in Lisbon at 8:30 in the morning. There in the airport we stood, with our luggage all around us, feeling lost. Portugal was a foreign land with a strange tongue. Would we be able to find our way to the hotel without taking a taxi? Who would help us, and guide us safely through these strange lands? We remembered our travel book. Arthur Frommer, author of Touring at $5 and $10 a Day, had said the bus was 7.5 escudios, as compared to 50 for a taxi. So naturally we took the airport bus. We quickly learned, that when in doubt, to consult the travel book immediately. Arthur became our expert guide whose wisdom sheltered us from much trouble.

Finally bag and baggage, we arrived at the Hotel Rex in Lisbon. They quickly showed us to our room. Oblivious to our surroundings, we merely dropped our suitcases on the floor and just collapsed onto the comfortable beds. We were that exhausted. Around noon, however, hunger pangs awakened me, but Lorraine couldn't or wouldn't stir. So I bravely trudged out to bring home not the "bacon", but the "bread and cheese." Down the hotel steps and to the left. Then a block or so to a small shop. It catered to hardworking clientele. In spite of the handicap of language, I soon was paying for my purchases of bread, cheese, and oranges. Back to the hotel where, to my dismay, I found I had left the cheese on the counter.

Retracing my footsteps to the delicatessen, I spotted my cheese wrapped and reposing in state on a high shelf. But the man, who had waited on me, had left for the day. No one could understand the connection between that particular cheese and me! Finally, thinking he knew, the clerk cut another identical piece of cheese for me. For which I paid and hurried back, feeling more like "Alice Lost in Wonderland" than a princess at the king's hotel. However, from these staples, Lorraine fashioned an adequate and delicious repast.

Fortified, we sailed forth to explore our first European city. Lorraine felt very sure of herself as a guide because each of the cobble-stoned streets winding their way uphill toward Eduardo VI Park was of a different mosaic design. When we reached the top of the Park, the city lay open before us: concrete high-rises, and red-tiled medieval buildings; Lisbon of the days of discoveries, and modern struggling Lisbon. Castilo S. Jorge, the Moorish stronghold, dominated the hillside close to the bay on one side of the city. But a nearby monument depicting Portuguese people at work seemed better to convey the spirit of their country to us: poor, struggling, hardworking, and pulling themselves back up by their bootstraps, so to speak.

As we walked through the Jardin Botanco, Lorraine picked a leaf as our very first souvenir of our trip. We felt so close

13

to the people of Portugal for the spirit of the country spoke to our hearts.

Back at the Hotel Rex on Rua Castilho, we turned in early, for tomorrow would be our very long tour (11 hours in fact) to Fatima. However, as we lay back in our beds, we relived the sights of Lisbon, noting the signs of their struggles. Even our hotel room had one wall sadly in need of repair and yet there was fabulous marble in the bathroom! We later learned that this was due to the nation's accommodating over a half million Angolan refugees in 1975. The government housed them indiscriminately in all the country's hotels. Surely this was a viable democratic ideal at work to solve a need.

Just how we managed to arise early enough to catch the Grayline Tour #1 for the 8:12 pickup at the Rex, was a miracle in itself. This was Wednesday, June 15th, and here we were pilgrims on the way to Fatima. The motor coach rolled past small farms on secondary roads. The entire countryside looked as if life was a constant struggle of survival. Past peach and apricot orchards into the town of Alcobaca, we were driven. Here we caught our breath in the simple, sheer beauty of the abbey church of the Monastery of Santa Maria built by the Cistercians in 1152. It was our first introduction to this type of exquisite beauty. Our American churches are so drab when compared to this little house of God.

We were now about 75 miles from Lisbon and the driver soon herded us, his tourists, into a restaurant at Leiria. It was a homey place. The soup was excellent and so was the chicken. Little did we know then that chicken was the main dish on all tourist tours!

Fatima was soon close at hand and we were glad to be alighting from the bus parked in front of the usual "tourist trap" store. However, once into the grounds of the Fatima shrine, the sights and sounds of commercialism dropped away. The quiet walkway wound among shade trees and then opened out onto a huge plaza. At the far end, the enormous Basilica loomed. Buildings flanked the two sides, built I presumed, to remind one of St. Peter's. The quiet and reverence at Fatima was remarkable. We prayed the Rosary at the outside shrine and lit one of the melting wax candles that were bending in the hot sun. All of our loved ones across the miles were united with us in spirit as our hearts expanded in love at Holy Communion time in the great Basilica dedicated to Mary. The power of simple faith is a cable that draws its strength from many strains of love. Of such is Fatima.

Ten miles to the west is a lovely monastery and cathedral to Our Lady of Victory, built in the 14th and 15th centuries. It is said to be the finest Gothic structure on the Iberian Peninsula and we could well believe this. The corridors were vistas of peace and beauty. It took no effort to see with the mind's eye: monks living, praying, and working for the Lord in that setting.

Westward to the sea dashed our bus. Then it stopped abruptly at the top of a 300 foot cliff! We dismounted to view the curve of the blue sea and the tiny fishing village below us. The villagers' fishing boats are curved high, both at bow and stern, to enable them to cut through the foaming breakers. The local costume of tartan-like design is supposed to date back to some shipwrecked Scotsmen on this coast centuries ago. A stocking cap was also used as the common head gear for the fishermen in the past. But we saw only one man wearing such a cap. At the present time, the village of Nazare' probably fishes more from tourists than from the ocean. But there is no doubt that the primitive strength and dignity of Portugal came from fishermen such as these who dared and conquered the sea.

The road back to Lisbon led through the water-meadows of Ribatejo where bulls are raised to fight. However, we saw only one bull grazing peacefully. He reminded us of "Ferdinand among the flowers." The bus returned us tired and happy to the Hotel Rex at 20:00 hours (8 p.m. to the unsophisticated). What an eventful day it had been!

CHAPTER IV
THE SOPHISTICATION AND GRANDEUR OF SPAIN

A 9:30 TWA morning flight from Lisbon found us at Madrid airport at 11:30 a.m. We took the airport bus and then a cab which circled the same streets twice! Lorraine sternly mentioned this and the driver quickly delivered us to our hotel. Our 7th floor room at the Florida Norte Hotel Residencia overlooks the river toward the west. As the hotel is on the edge of Madrid, trees and hills stretch out before our gaze. However, the street immediately below us bordering the river is lined with highrise hotels and apartment buildings such as the one we are in now. From our window we watched hundreds of swallows darting from their nests and circling about in droves. These are the permanent residents who live in their mud penthouses high under the eves of the hotels.

Just a short walk from our Residencia enabled us to catch the bus into town for sightseeing. Madrid is a most beautiful city: glorious fountains, lovely parks, and tall marble buildings (spoiled in their grandeur by political signs plastered like wallpaper on the lovely walls). Our destination was the Prada which is jam-packed with art treasures. We drank in El Greco's, Velazquez's, Murillo's, Ribera's and Goya's until it became too much for our human frames. We staggered outside and collapsed on the lawn. Jet-lag had caught up with us. Lorraine promptly was asleep. I would have been also, except I thought one of us should remain awake and be on guard in a foreign city. My mind wandered and I pondered how really strange it was that the two of us would be on a lawn outside this magnificent museum in Spain. There slept Lorraine, young, vivacious, a real people-person, eager to meet and know the stranger. There was myself, older by 15 years, quiet, studious, more interested in nature and scenery. I had a thought, if there were transmigration of souls, perhaps Lorraine would come back as a Spanish lady in this city and I would come back as a Portuguese peasant on a farm. After all, Lorraine had chosen WOMEN IN MATTHEW as her thesis topic and that gospel was written for the more comfortable city dwellers. While I, identifying with the gospel of Mark written for the peasants and lower-class artisans living in small towns and villages in the rural countryside of a Roman occupied province, had written about WOMEN IN MARK.

After an hour or so, Lorraine awoke and we headed back to our rooms. Once there, a beautiful display of nature awaited us. The setting sun was touching the dark cloud formations with gold and purple fingers. Then the night became velvety dark and only the three stars in Orion's Belt shone bright to bid us rest well on this our first night in Spain.

The next day, Friday June 17th, was another, crammed full to the brim and running over, adventuresome day. Up in the early dawn, with a continental breakfast, (we ate every roll in sight) and then a race out the door to hop aboard a city bus to land hopefully somewhere near the tour bus terminal. This just happened to be located elusively in some tiny obscure side street off Jose Antonio Avenue. However, Lorraine, with her San Antonio Texas Spanish, first asked a policeman for directions which took us part of the way. Next Lorraine questioned a young girl. We turned and hurried down another street. Finally Lorraine added arm gestures to her Spanish, causing a very helpful older woman with an alert police dog to walk with us a pace. A turn, a pointing gesture, and behold at 8:25 a.m. we were actually sitting in the tour bus!

At 8:30 sharp, the driver skillfully maneuvered his lumbering monster out of its stall, edging by other still sleeping denizens waiting to devour their load of eager tourists. Past office buildings, smart shops, and palatial villas with park-like grounds, we rolled. The bus headed northwest across the high plateau and into the rolling hills. The terrain resembled Wyoming, for the trees were short and stunted, due to the elevation. Two high ridges of mountains rose up in the distance. We were headed toward the Valley of the Fallen. Here Spain honors all the dead from both sides of their civil war. A tunnel was drilled straight into the rock heart of the mountain 1,300 meters above sea level. One walks into the entrance-way and the atmosphere awes you into respectful silence for the 80,000 people that lie buried here. Each light fixture bears the design of shroud and wreath. Beautiful modern icons of the Annunciation and various episodes in the life of Christ are fastened on to the granite walls. The vaulted roof of rough-hewn granite stretched high above us in the dim light. As we walked softly down the 300 meters toward the main altar, we passed enormous statues of Mary depicted in various ways as patroness for different branches of the nation's armed forces.

Four long, dark tunnels run out like the arms of a double cross from the huge sanctuary. Within their walls, the dead lie interred. The cross on the main altar stretches upward and is made from a single tree. Four enormous angels stand silent guard. Hidden behind the altar, a choir stall can be glimpsed. Benedictine monks who live on the other side of the mountain, descend unseen into the church by back elevator to chant prayers for the country's dead. High above the altar, the dome consists of a gigantic mosaic of 30,000 pieces which depicts the souls of the dead marching toward Christ carrying their army, navy or other armed forces banner aloft. The thought of so many fallen in civil war is heart rendering.

From the floor to the top of the dome measured 300 meters. Outside on the mountain and directly above, stands another cross raising its granite arms up another 300 meters. This cross is visible 20 miles away. The four evangelists stand at the base. Smaller figures representing the "Virtues" are carved higher up on the pedestal. Shrines commemorating the Way of the Cross depict a path of suffering on the surrounding mountains. This shadowy church or mausoleum is a place of solemn beauty, and a place of reverence for the dead, to promote the cause for peace and to reunite the people of Spain. The Valley of the Fallen overwhelms one with a sense of our own mortality.

Back in the sunshine outside, our bus glided down the mountainside and into the El Escorial. This is a large, rectangular complex containing rooms for the king and his family, courtyards, a cloister for the monks who tend the church and gardens, and with the church itself in the middle. It was built like a gridiron in honor of St. Lawrence by Philip II. (Philip, who was very austere and, living in the culture of the 15th century, wanted to remind his family of the martyrdom of St. Lawrence.) Also within the complex, there is a special room in which the bones of the kings and the queen mothers of Spain are encased in magnificent black marble caskets arranged around the sides of the tomb. The effect was quite somber. Rather morbid, we thought. Wouldn't want to be Philip's wife.

After so much darkness and death, we were more than ready for sunshine and a lighter side of life. Luckily the afternoon had quite a different atmosphere than the morning as we motored south to Toledo. This ancient walled town is now preserved as a national monument. The main attraction is the fabulous woodwork in the Cathedral. Behind the main altar, the entire back panel contains thousands of statues and symbols molded in gold and silver. The choir itself stands in the middle of the church with its carved choir seats and arm rests while two organs, one in baroque and one in renaissance style, loom overhead. The Treasury of the Cathedral contains many beautiful articles. The most unique of all (in our opinion) was a monstrance about six feet high and shaped like a gothic cathedral. Each of thousands of figures in its canopy can be unscrewed and lifted out. It took 19 years for the Dutch-German artist to carve the whole masterpiece. Such a long labor of devotion! The thought was overwhelming to us!

In the nearby church of San Tomas is a magnificent painting by El Greco portraying the death of the Duke of Toledo and of his soul being helped into Heaven by the Blessed Virgin Mary and St. Peter. St. Augustine and another saint are at his bedside. If the duke needed this extra help to get to heaven, I wonder how much more help would be needed for our own politicians!

A little human sidelight after so much spirituality. We lunched at a restaurant high on a hill overlooking the town. Surprise... the menu was exactly the same as the one at Fatima: chicken, potatoes, and pudding!

On the morning of Saturday, the 18th, we leisurely packed, got ourselves together, and checked out of the hotel. Then we attended High Mass in Our Lady of Mt. Carmel Basilica in downtown Madrid. The liturgy lasted two hours and we couldn't understand a word. However, the organ filled the church with music and the male singer had a grand voice. All this for the two of us and 28 other people! My Mom, with her love of the Carmelites, would have felt quite at home in that church with its dressed statues of Our Lady of Mt. Carmel. No, the plural is no mistake. There were two statues!

After Mass we walked about a bit, finally collected our luggage and headed straight into the chaos of the Madrid airport. By 4:20 p.m. though, we were looking out the windows of Iberia 577 flying over the five million people crowding the streets and highrises of Madrid. It is a very well planned and beautiful city with its parks and fountains. Madridites are well dressed and sophisticated. Spain has such a different culture from that of Portugal where the people are really poor, hardworking, and earnestly striving to pull themselves up economically. Theirs is simple, homey friendliness. But Spain has glamour! No doubt about that!

Our plane flew over the high, dry plateau and finally over hillsides covered with olive trees. We landed at a tiny airport in Granada with only one bus that headed back into town. It was Saturday night, only about 6:25 p.m. when we discovered this fact. Granada must roll up its sidewalks at twilight for everything, even the tourist office, was closed! Finally, in despair, we asked a cab driver to take us to the Parador Nacional De San Francisco. This was to be our very own special abode on the grounds of the Alhambra. Once the Parador was part of a very old convent monastery. Beautiful paintings on the wall depicted the life of St. Francis. We dined in state and then returned to our room. There we found that our beds were turned down and the beautiful white bedspreads placed carefully to one side. Glimpses of the Alhambra proper were to be seen through the open window as we drifted into sleep cradled in the lap of luxury.

The next morning, Sunday, dawned bright and joy-filled. We walked next door and into a huge church with high brick walls. The altar, the sides, the steps, every nook and cranny were alive with blooming roses. A beautiful bride with her mother, and the groom with his father, knelt at the foot of the altar. It was a glorious nuptial mass on the Feast of Corpus Christi. Who would not rejoice with this young couple?

After wishing the couple God's special blessings on their wedding day and in the years yet to come, we walked out of the church and entered the lovely palace and grounds of the Alhambra. The thousand love stories of the Moorish princess seem to fill the very air. Tales of the Alhambra that I had read as a child became alive as I retold the stories to Lorraine there on the grounds of the Alhambra. Then as night drew on, a cab driver took us over to the other side of town and up, up a narrow winding road with white-washed walls grazing the sides of the car. There in the churchyard at the top, we gazed in awe at the golden glow of the lights shining on the ancient walls of the Alhambra. Transfixed, we stood drinking in the bewitching beauty of the Alhambra. We were deep into a fairy tale experience at that very moment.

However, with the dawning of a new day, harsh realities can return. And it so happened that we also crashed back to earth in the experiences of the following day. Up at 6 a.m. in order to catch the train (a commuter electric streetcar) at 8:30 from Granada to Babadilla. The coach was filled with men and their work tools. We were quite out of place for two reasons: we were the only women there, and second, we had too much heavy luggage. Enough said! For two hours the train lumbered along through rolling hills covered either with hay fields or dotted with olive trees. The custom in this region is to cut off the tops of the trees and to allow the side branches to grow long. Thus the fruit can be picked from the ground. What a very practical idea, I thought. I wonder why we aren't using this method in our orchards? From the train window, we found it sometimes difficult to distinguish the distant olive groves from the closer vineyards. Occasionally a stark granite rock formation jutted up on a hillside like a sentinel on watch.

At Babadilla I had to buy tickets for Cordoba. Finally, I had caught on to the benefit of writing out our destination, as no one spoke English and neither could they understand my attempted pronunciation of the Spanish names. At 10:59 we piled onto the train and, to our dismay, found that our luggage was obviously in everyone's way. We shared first the tiny compartment with three young men. Undaunted, they quickly threw our suitcases up onto the high overhead racks. After they reached their destination, we moved over to their window seats to enjoy the scenery that resembled our own California but with a lot more "Atmosphere": stone forts, and ruins of various types crowning the sunny hilltops, thrown into the mix.

About half an hour outside of Cordoba, we decided it was time to get the luggage down for our own departure. Lorraine struggled to pull down the tightly wedged suitcases. Finally, we succeeded in this momentous task. But just as we had collapsed back into our seats exhausted, our tiny compartment was invaded again. This time by one man, three women, and two lively youngsters who looked at our luggage piled in the center in frank amazement. The five of them were traveling with only a plastic bag! We were more than a little embarrassed.

At long last, the train puffed into Cordoba at 1:07 with its hot, tired, and squashed human cargo! We had thought perhaps someone might help us, but no! Everyone rushed out of the train at exactly the same moment a new crowd was rushing in. The train steps, to make matters worse, resembled a steep ladder propped against the side of the coach. As I neared the doorway, a stranger threw a heavy suitcase onto the train, completely blocking the aisle and smashing my toes. This galvanized me into action! "Here," I cried, dropping down to him our suitcases as fast as Lorraine frantically dragged them out of the crowded compartment. His reflexes were superb and within minutes we were standing on the platform alongside our luggage mound. We carefully made no comment because we hadn't as yet distanced ourselves enough from the horrible train ride to be able to see the humor in our situation.

Checking our suitcases, we set out in the blazing heat for the Mesquita de Cordoba. We walked and walked until we thought we would drop. Finally we staggered through an ancient courtyard up to the very doorway of this huge, old church only to find it locked! Closed for the long siesta. Not to be opened until 4 p.m. We did have a choice; either miss our next train or miss seeing the church built inside an ancient mosque. The die was cast. Decide! Well, not for so many thousands of miles had we come here to see this wonder to give up too easily! We adjusted, found a stone curbing to sit on beneath a shade tree in the courtyard, and wrote letters home. As we scribbled away, a couple, whom we had met climbing the Fortress of the Alhambra, walked by taking pictures. We greeted them like long-lost cousins. Any fellow countryman is like a glimpse of home in a foreign land.

Finally our patient wait was rewarded and we walked inside the building. No, not a building really, but a forest of slender columns and arches decorated with red strips stretching into infinity in every direction. What dainty beauty assailed our senses. Then there, in the middle of these Moorish trees, arose an immense baroque Christian church! The solid walnut back of the altar was heavily carved and trimmed with gold. The choir was a high square with carved dark wood stalls and lofty organs edged with gold and silver. Around the edges of this amazing Mosque/Cathedral were side chapels, each with its own paintings and richly dressed statues. Seeing this unique Mosque/Cathedral was for us more than worth the troubles of missing a train.

Out once more into the brilliant sunshine, we trudged wearily back to the station. Along the way, three young men joined us for a while. They were traveling on a shoestring also. Still when I breathed out how tired I was, the boy next to me said he would carry me to the station for a quarter! I laughingly refused. But then I reached into my pocket, and drew out some Spanish coins. "Here," I said, "see what you can do with this." He turned and dashed off into a nearby bakery. And returned with the longest, skinniest loaf of bread I ever saw. Breaking it in half, he handed a portion to me.

So Lorraine and I each broke off a tiny piece from it. We were much more thirsty than hungry. I handed back our half and the young man said, "If you insist..." Two minutes later, the three had that whole long loaf polished off. Then they spotted something that looked like a secondhand junkyard down a side street and waving goodbye, they loped away. We continued along our hot and dusty way toward the train station. Each could read the complete exhaustion stamped on the other's sweating face. Our scheduled train had long gone. Therefore, we bought another ticket for Seville. While waiting, we quenched our thirst with a cold drink at a little open-air cafe facing the railroad station's courtyard. Our train was due at 6:35 p.m. but 6:35 came and went as we paced back and forth anxiously on Track #1's platform. As the hands of the big clock moved toward 7 p.m., our agitation became more and more noticeable. But the trainmen kept assuring us. "Train, Seville, Track 1, soon." At 7:15 a sleek train darted into the station. A porter swung our luggage up and practically lifted us aboard. He motioned frantically for a tip as we found ourselves sinking back into deep, individual plush seats in a luxurious parlor car. Huge picture windows enabled us to view men and women working in the fields while their little donkeys were waiting to plod homeward in the evening twilight with their loaded panniers.

Five minutes out of Cordoba, trouble came in the form of the conductor. Looking at our tickets, he burst into rapid Spanish and shook his head vigorously. I was scared. Were we headed in the wrong direction after all that wait? But Lorraine, being a better judge of human nature than I, surmised that a little extra money would solve the problem of second-class fares in first-class seats! So we opened our purse to the conductor and relaxed in this beautiful air-conditioned train- -our first experience with the famous T-T-E trains of Europe. This marvel clipped off the miles and reached Seville in an hour, passing up our poor old second-class train that had been huffing and puffing along for over two hours.

We alighted at St. Bernardo Station in style. However, all the taxis were on strike. Finally the hotel grudgingly sent a car and it cost us dearly. Next, the Registrar at the hotel was quite arrogant. Lorraine commented, "We don't have to take that." So after a refreshing bath, we walked out into the evening and found a tiny family hotel just a stone's throw away. As soon as morning came, we trundled our luggage out the front door of the Colon Hotel and up the street to be taken under the wing of the family at our new tiny pension. The owners were so pleasant and courteous. Their youngster, about ten, was trying so hard to be grown up as he dusted, served, handed your key to you, etc.

This was now Tuesday, June 21st, and we had slept very late because of the exhausting train ride from Granada. However, after settling into our new hotel, Londes, we walked over to the Great Cathedral of Seville. It covers at least two square blocks, and we spent over three hours just looking around inside. This is the largest Gothic building in the world and it contains numerous chapels inside. We attended Mass in the Chapel of Ferdinand III with his royal silver casket resting in state nearby. In the background, there was a statue of Mary and Child, dressed as royalty. Alabaster statues near the altar depicted the Spanish king and queen praying. Silver abounded everywhere in the church.

We were not yet finished viewing the church when the guards actually put us out at 1:30. That siesta hour again! So we explored the Garden of Queen Maria Luisa nearby. Our hungry appetites gave us the excuse to sit at an open-air cafe and watch some very young French sailors self-consciously stroll by. Just an interesting sidelight; we have seen more policemen and other members of the armed forces here on a single normal day than we have ever seen in an entire year in the U.S. Soldiers are just everywhere. Some with machine guns were even guarding doorways. For what reason, we had no idea.

Finally, wornout by sightseeing, we turned our steps back to our pleasant tiny hotel Londes and were asleep by 9 p.m.

Wednesday-- up and packed. We formally checked out, but our dear lady at the Londes put our luggage in the back of the desk so we could go sightseeing unhampered.

Off to the Church of St. Mary Magdalene for Mass. Most impressive of all was their Chapel of the Blessed Sacrament with perpetual adoration. The Chapel's tabernacle and the monstrance resembled a sunburst of brightest glory. There were also many interesting paintings in this church.

We returned to the Great Cathedral to finish seeing the king's treasures. (Yesterday a rude woman had shuttered and locked the cases right in our faces.) So today we finished seeing everything we had missed. Then we were off to the Alcazar. This was a fortress palace. The Arabs were masters at using the concept of light, air, water, gardens, and plumbing even before the 10th century. Next we followed the narrow, winding streets of the Barrio Santa Cruz. Balconies jutted over our heads with hanging flowers. We caught glimpses of cool indoor patios with splashing fountains, potted plants, and abounding with much decorative tile.

We checked out the University of Seville, walked up the marble staircases, and sauntered down the long halls lined with statues. But their classrooms still had the same old familiar look as ours: blackboards, scruffy chairs, etc. We could teach here and think it was a school at home.

Feeling starved, we started back towards the Londes. But alert to the flow of pedestrians, Lorraine piloted us up some stairs in the wake of a hurrying crowd and into a cafeteria. It was about 2:30 p.m. and our lunch lasted quite a while. In fact, when we did finally quit eating, we felt just like Gorda, fat and stuffed!

Our real problem was that basically not knowing the local custom, we kept mistaking each course as the main one. As soon as we cleaned our plate, another full course popped up in front of us. After this cafe experience, we could scarcely wobble back to the hotel.

In truth, in all of Spain we ate exceptionally well. A little too well, in fact, except for the train ride day when we missed all of our meals. However, if we had to vote for the best and the most unforgettable meal in Spain, we would vote for the Alhambra: a beautiful view, a luxurious setting and delicious food. The first course was a soup made of fresh vegetables and cold tomatoes, the second was a mixed vegetable and fish dish, the third swordfish and pork chops, the fourth fresh fruit and pastry! At least 10 stars!

Time to leave Seville. No airportobus, so we had to take a cab to the airport. Instead of the 8:10 p.m. plane, we walked straight onto the earlier one. However, the airplane ran into a strange looking high shelf of clouds. Our luck was changing again! By the time the plane arrived at Barcelona, we were already 45 minutes late. Then the ferrocar that took the air passengers into the city center refused to move. Perhaps the electricity was off due to the storm and lightning. Finally, when the other ferrocar returned from its 7.5 mile run into Barcelona, everyone was transferred into it. Once in Barcelona proper, Lorraine decided we would take the Metro to our hotel. The gate-man did not speak English, but a lovely German girl happened by. She listened, translated into half German and Spanish, retranslated to Lorraine, and we started on our way only to have the girl frantically call us back. She had been directing us to the Holy Family Church instead of the Great Cathedral! With the new set of instructions, Lorraine dashed confidently into the maze of stairs, cars, tubes, on and off, change cars, run, run. I could scarcely keep up. It was only the fear of being left alone in a strange madhouse that kept me going. At long last the right station was reached. Up a short flight of stairs to the street. Oh no, a torrent of water was pouring down the subway steps! We waited a while but, as the storm did not seem to abate in the least, we ventured up the stairs and out into the downpour. After all, we thought, we have only a block and a half to go to the Great Cathedral and our hotel is directly across the street from the church.

Nevertheless, by the time we reached the hotel, we looked like poor, drenched, little orphans of the storm. There we stood dripping from head to foot in the plush hall of the ultra luxurious Hotel Colon. I am sure they had never seen the likes of us before. The management quickly moved us off their Persian rugs and into our own rooms. There the attentive maid kept bringing extra towels and helping us dry our wet clothes. After hot baths and drying off with great towels bigger than we were, we were safely tucked into our comfortable beds around midnight. We will always look back with gratitude to that kind and solicitous woman who took such motherly care of us poor, bedraggled creatures.

How sad we thought as we tried to drag ourselves out of bed the next morning in Room 208, how sad that we had so little time in this fabulous hotel. Nevertheless, we hurriedly crossed the street for Mass in the Chapel of Christ the Pardoner within this Great Cathedral of Cristo Rey. This was a functioning parish Church and not just a museum. A very hopeful sign of faith, we thought. There were stairs in the middle of the nave which we descended to the crypt of St. Eulalia to say a prayer for our own Sister Eulalia at home.

This Colon Hotel in Barcelona was "the" top-notch hotel we had stayed in so far in our journey. (In fact, it would remain #1 for our entire trip.) The Colon even had the special soap that Lorraine's Mom liked so well. It has been amazing to us how well we, two inexperienced travelers, have managed so far. Lorraine's friendly manner and her smattering of Spanish has helped to smooth out many difficulties. We will never forget how willing the Spanish people were to walk out of their way to lead us to the Post Office, or Museum, or Cathedral.

But Iberian planes and trains were definitely another matter altogether. They were disorganized chaos-- just a clutter and a push of crowding people. But astonishingly, one does manage to get on. Then one sits exhausted as we did in our Iberian DC9 waiting for takeoff at 11 a.m. on June 23rd.

Straight across the Mediterranean for 1,200 miles, the plane skimmed above the water and then up over a solid looking cloud bank. At our top speed of 650 miles, it will take us two hours to reach Rome, but it will still only be 11:40 a.m. Our hostesses gave us cold meat and tea for lunch. It was cool when we left Barcelona. In fact, we have had perfect weather this whole trip so far. Who can complain about one torrential downpour in ten days?

Just looked down and we are flying over the huge island of Sardinia with its very rugged coastline. Now only blue water again until we touch down at Rome's airport.

Rome's airport is large but we could not go outside the terminal because we were due to embark on TWA 848 at 3:40 p.m. for Tel Aviv.

As we waited, we became surrounded by a group of elderly ladies who were on a pilgrimage from Buffalo to Jerusalem. Lorraine struck up a lively conversation with the priest, who was shepherding this flock of pilgrims, and he invited us to join with them on the taxi ride to the Holy City. The last lap of our journey to the Holy Land thus finally began as we board the plane to Tel Aviv.

LUCILLE HINTZE

CHAPTER V
ISRAEL - JUNE 23RD TO JULY 26TH

As the plane took off from Rome on our last lap to the Promised Land, the fact that God had provided such a friendly and fatherly priest willing to include us with his group helped immensely. We did have one Real Worry. We had not heard whether or not the Franciscan Sisters were able to accommodate us. Without a bed in a strange land is a Problem! Then too, ours was an afternoon TWA flight starting at 3:40 p.m. and arriving at 6:45 p.m. which meant it would be quite dark. Not a good time to be wandering around.

No sooner had we landed at the Lod airport, than a strange man grabbed our luggage and rushed out, straight through Customs, with us running frantically after him! As soon as we were outside the building, the shouting mob of people stretching from the lighted area into the darkness beyond, frightened us even more. We grabbed our luggage out of the man's hands to his amazement and consternation, and, pushing a path through the crowd rushing out, fought our way back inside. Once within the safety of the building, we waited quietly to one side until Father and his little flock were reassembled. Father then negotiated for two "Sherut" taxicabs. These are "7+1" Mercedes limousines that carry people everywhere. After the price is negotiated, each passenger pays his/her share. Later we wondered at seeing so many Mercedes-Benz machines in Israel. Even the old Arab buses were Mercedes. Two reasons, we discovered, were the cause of this phenomena. The first was that Germany needed to make reparations to the Jews, so the Mercedes were offered at cost. And second, Mercedes engines were about the only engines made that could stand up under the extreme heat and road conditions in Israel. Most of the drivers of the "Sheruts" are independents and their taxi is usually family owned. They also drive very fast and casually as if they were the best drivers in the world.

The road from Lod to Jerusalem is pleasant and winds upwards into the hills. Forests are beginning to make their comeback on the rocky hillsides, due to Israel's 'plant a tree' program. The entire country had been denuded of every tree during the time of the Turkish occupation. Some trees were cut for the railroads. The rest were taxed out of existence. Families could not afford to pay the high tax on their olive trees.

However, most of this was not evident to us on this particular night as our "Sherut" sped through the darkness to the pilgrim hotel of Father's group in Jerusalem. Once there, we telephoned the Franciscan Sisters. Yes, they had expected us. Soon we found ourselves in a tiny, but adequate room with two iron beds and, best of all, with our own shower. We were very fortunate!

The Franciscan Sisters, known in Jerusalem as the "White Sisters," numbered about 9,000 in the entire world. The hospice was filling as Sister-missionaries were arriving from all parts of the world: India, South Africa, Australia. Mother Jon Marie put a B.V.M. Sister and the two of us with a group of their own Sisters who spoke English. Judging by their accent, these Sisters were mainly British.

Thus our sojourn in the Holy Land began as we opened our eyes on June 24th halfway around the world from where we had studied the events of the life of Christ! An Arab bus rolled up to the door. The Franciscan Sisters and we got on for our journey to Ein Kirem, the home of Zachary and Elizabeth.

Arriving, we walked up the steep hillside path to the Church of the Visitation. Here in the courtyard, the Magnificat is spelled out in 50 different languages on the tile walls. "My soul magnifies the Lord and my spirit rejoices in God my Savior." (Luke 1:14f). We looked out over the countryside and were glad, for He who is mighty had done great things for us also. Then we carefully picked our way down the cobblestone path and across the road to the church commemorating the Birth of John the Baptist. Here we attended the special Mass in his honor concelebrated by 24 priests and the Bishop. The place was packed with Franciscans. Afterwards, one of the Franciscan Brothers took us under the church where we saw the pillars and mosaics of the first early church built here by St. Helena, mother of Constantine. But the spot had been singled out for use long before, as there was evidence underground of an even earlier, ancient, non-Christian temple there.

On our trip to Bethlehem with the sisters, we first visited the Franciscan Sisters' Convent there. The missionaries in our party received a very royal welcome. The Bethlehemites were also proud to show us their chapel which had lovely inlaid woodwork. This had been done by a Trappist hermit who, while doing the chapel restoration, had lived in a tiny hut on their grounds for three years.

In the afternoon we made our first visit to Bethlehem proper, the house of bread. The fortress-like church sits at one end of the square. The entrance door is small and low to the ground. One has to bend almost double in order to enter. This was to prevent the Turks from riding their horses into the church. Four rows of pinkish Corinthian pillars divided the interior. Each bears a picture, perhaps of the wise men and the apostles. But the Eastern dress of these Magi once saved the church from ruin. The Persians, when they saw the Magi, counted the Church of the Nativity as a holy place. Thus this particular church was spared from the destruction of all the other churches in the area. The present church, although the most ancient church in the Holy Land, is upon a site of another one built by Queen Helena. Here and there are trap doors in the floor so that you can view the ancient mosaics. The front altar is beautiful with decorations in gold leaf. Lamps are hanging everywhere. We walked around the right side of the altar and then down a narrow stone staircase into a cave. There, beneath a tiny simple altar, is a spot marked by a silver star. In the center of the star is a place where you can reach down and touch the ground of the place where Jesus was born. We knelt down and felt the thrill of touching this holy spot, as we prayed especially for our loved ones. To one side was the section where the original wooden Manger was supposed to have been. These cave walls were covered with tapestry to prevent the earthen walls from being literally carried away by the tourists! Even further underground are the caves where St. Jerome lived and wrote his translation of the Bible.

From Jerome's Cave there is also a very narrow passageway that leads upwards to the Cave of the Nativity. Back up the narrow stairs on the left side of the main altar, we passed quietly by the chanting Armenian priests. The Greek Orthodox are on the right side. We actually visited this church three times: first with the "White" Sisters, later with the class from Tantur, and last of all on our own walking pilgrimage.

That last time was the most strenuous of all! We had taken the ancient road from Jerusalem to Bethlehem that wound back of Tantur to the site of the Nativity and then out into the countryside to where the shepherds kept watch over their flocks. Only, foolishly, we were not making the journey in the cool of the night but in midday. In the blazing heat, we naturally became extremely hot. We wilted more and more as we walked through the dry grazing land to the site of the shepherds' cave.

Finally the road led through a stone archway and up a long driveway which wound around the small hill. Beneath this knoll, there was a large cave with visitors praying within. Above the shepherds' cave was a tiny chapel. Lorraine was so hot and tired; she didn't even want to climb the few remaining feet to visit this!

Then a Franciscan Brother at the chapel told us to our dismay that we would have to walk all the way back to Beit Sahour for a bus! A tiny wayside stand just outside the enclosed Shepherds' Field provided a cold drink to fortify us for this long trek back to the school.

The road stretched out longer, hotter, and dustier with every passing moment. True, there were Bedouins with donkeys (we wished we had one) plus sheep and goats grazing. But our sheer exhaustion kept us from enjoying the pastoral scene. Finally we arrived at the tiny village and climbed into a bus back to Bethlehem.

Because of this particular unhappy pilgrimage, we learned a vital lesson. It would be much better to take a bus or taxi first to the place we wanted to visit so that we would arrive refreshed at our destination and enjoy it. To arrive exhausted was very counterproductive to say the least!

Also in Israel, we learned the real value of the Biblical words concerning the washing of the feet. Such washing is one of the most necessary and one of the most refreshing actions one can do, especially after a long jaunt of five miles! We washed ours every time we staggered back exhausted to our rooms from walking. In addition, I would brush the dust from our shoes and wash them also. Thank God for our sandals! Our feet could breathe in the heat.

There are two sites that lay claim to be the "original Shepherds' Field" where the shepherds were resting in their cave on the night of Jesus' birth. The second Shepherds' Field was a very easy bus trip. The school bus from Tantur drove up to the gateway, we jumped out of the bus, walked past the grazing sheep and into a large cave. No strain!

We stayed with the Franciscan Sisters in Jerusalem from Thursday night until Sunday afternoon. Sister Flora proved a real friend when she realized that the "just tourist fare" was not enough for us. She not only recommended but helped us enroll into Tantur. What a blessing that was! It really made our whole Israel experience.

The real title for our school was The Ecumenical Institute for Advanced Theological Studies. It is located on a hill known as Tantur, which is just off the main road between Jerusalem and Bethlehem. The word Tantur means something "that stands up like the hump of a camel." Its 35-acre campus is covered with 400 olive trees. The driveway winds up the hill and then through a very narrow gateway erected by the Knights of Malta in 1868. In fact it is so narrow that cars have to draw in their sides to avoid scratching the paint! Once inside, though, the buildings are new and modern. The library complex is to the right and the monastery of the Benedictine Monks from Monteserrat, Spain, to the left. Dead center is the main building with the administrative offices, rooms, and in the back the dining room. This place was the brainchild of Pope John the 23rd and the 2nd Vatican Council. The governing board is 1/3 Protestant, 1/3 Catholic, and 1/3 Orthodox. Its purpose is to focus on biblical and theological studies in relationship to biblical history, geography and archaeology. This idea of experiencing the Holy Land within a context of planned study and travel was an absolutely perfect situation for us.

We took an Arab bus on Sunday to enroll as students at Tantur. That Sunday also, we attended the concelebrated Mass of two Maryknoll priests who were students at the school. In the early evening, we returned to stay at Tantur for the summer session. Dr. Walter Wegner, director of the Institute, had made quite a concession for us. The limit of students there was usually only 30. But the two of us made 31. One too many! We were very happy that Dr. Wegner waved the rule and allowed us to enroll. Here at Tantur, we each had our own room with a connecting bath. Our windows were sliding doors that looked to the Southeast. The food was excellent-- tasty Arab cooking. We learned quickly to like goat yogurt, many different kinds of cheese, and various unguessable combinations of stuff wrapped in grape leaves.

On the intellectual side, we had courses and lectures given by Professor Shalom Ben-Chorin, Fr. Michele Piccirillo, Dr. Saul Colbi, Dean Ted Todd, Dr. Walter Wegner, Prof. Ora Lipschitz, Prof. Yiannis Meimaris, Dr. David Noel Freedman, Dr. Albert Glock, Ms. Martha Rittmeijer, Dr. Geoffrey Wigoder, Fr. Bargel Pixner, Dr. Hava Lazarus-Yafeh, Emahoy Krestos Samra, Mr. Yusef Saad, Mayor Elias Freij and Mr. Dennis Young. Fr. Michele Piccirillo turned out to be the driest lecturer of all for he was almost too knowledgeable in his subject. Ora Lipschitz was the liveliest and most interesting in the way she presented her material.

It was fairly easy to visit the Holy Places in Bethlehem from Tantur. We used the old Roman Road that Mary and Joseph must have taken from Jerusalem to Bethlehem. Twice from the Church of the Nativity, we walked up Manger Street, passed shops making carvings from olive wood, to the Milk Grotto. Part of the rock forming this grotto is of a milky white color, hence the name. Milk Grotto is a small wayside shrine surrounding a cave where the Holy Family paused for rest on their flight to Egypt. Inside is a lovely statue-group, with Joseph leading the donkey, on which Mary rides holding the Infant in her arms. It is very difficult to get into the shrine to see the Milk Grotto, for there is only one Franciscan Brother in charge and he is often on duty elsewhere. It was remarkable that we even succeeded on the second try.

On impulse, while returning to Tantur from one of our infamous hot and dusty excursions, we decided to cut across the fields to visit the Benedictine Sisters. The ground was rough going. Plus we were not quite sure of the way. When we stopped to ask directions from an Arab family, their ferocious dog wanted to make mincemeat out of us! Fortunately he was stoutly chained or he would have eaten us alive. Having reached the Benedictine Convent, we admired the sisters' exquisite embroidery work. We did succumb to temptation and bought some material from the Sisters. (Not that we needed any more stuff to carry!) But Lorraine had her dress made locally and it looked very attractive on her. However,

I thought buying a couple of straw hats in Bethlehem much more practical. We do differ in our tastes.

From the hill at Tantur we could look across the plain and see in the distance a cone-shaped mountain looking like someone had neatly sliced off the top. This was the Herodion, one of the fortresses of Herod the Great. We actually climbed down into this cone and explored the ruins on June 19th. Frankly, we were always very glad for our school trips. Fr. Piccirello had been lecturing upon the various ages, starting from 500,000 B.C. to King Herod. It was indeed too much, too fast, for our intellectual digestion. Therefore, we needed to wander a bit like the Patriarchs of old with their flocks. Like Amos, the prophet, who stirred up a hornet's nest, we buzzed over the rough ground among the sheep in the Tekoa Region. We bent over the deep cisterns and shuddered at the thought of all the labor required just to haul up enough water for those many roving sheep, each branded with different colored stripes on their wool.

On one of our trips with Ora over the mountainous back road to Jericho, we passed by Herod's winter palace straddling one of the streams that flow from the mountains to water the fertile valley of Jericho. We remember Herod because he sought to kill the Child, Jesus; but that was actually just least of the great king's many crimes. Herod killed his wife, whom he claimed to love, and also several of his sons. The Roman Emperor Augustine remarked that it was safer to be Herod's pig than his son. Herod was definitely NOT a loving family man!

Jericho is one of the oldest, if not the oldest, city in the world. Excavations have laid bare 23 different strata, the oldest of which is 10,000 years old. Out we tumbled from the school bus like obedient school children, and followed Ora up the sandy, rocky hillside. We looked down at the various archaeological excavations, the most interesting of which was a high, round stone tower dating from the Neolithic period. It must have been for cultic purposes because it was solid. Therefore, it could not be a fortress. Whether the walls of Jericho tumbled down for Joshua or at an earlier age, Jericho had always been a very strategic place because it is located in an extremely fertile oasis.

For ourselves this day, we were glad to cross the road from the ruins to a colorful, shady inn opposite to cool down a mite. Nearby was a bubbling, clear pool of water flowing refreshingly by. Children were having fun wading there. This is Elisha's Fountain where the prophet threw salts into the polluted waters to make them pure. This cool, sweet water is still drinkable today.

For our special own "desert experience" with Ora, the school bus left Tantur in the early morning, 6:30 a.m. in fact. Once we passed Bethany, the road winds through hot and arid mountains. The road workers on the new highway had contoured the passes so that the pastel-toned streaks of rose, pink, orange, and soft greens in the bordering rock walls could be seen. This is an artistic touch our highways might well copy. This was once an ancient caravan route, then an old Roman road, and the ruins of an aqueduct still run parallel to the now modern highway. We stopped at the spot where the Good Samaritan's Inn might have been. There are Roman and Turkish ruins there now.

Although the drive from Jerusalem to Jericho now takes only an hour, it is really still "down to Jericho," because you start at 2,700 feet above sea level and descend to 1,300 feet below sea level! It was strange to pass a sign saying "sea level" with dry, stony mountains on either side of your bus. Once we were down into the Jordan Valley, we took the left fork to Jericho. On this last hot stretch of highway, we passed on the left an abandoned refugee camp with hundreds of desolate, drab, one-room huts. This was once the largest refugee village in Jordan and quite a contrast to the tree-lined fertile lands of Jericho itself. (These camps fostered much bitterness among the Arabs and it is easy to understand why.)

Our class also visited the mosaic floor of a first-century synagogue and another mosaic of the Byzantine era. The first was under an Arab house. The mosaic was discovered while excavating for the foundation of the house. However, the Bureau of Antiquities does not allow such discoveries to be destroyed. Still the builder needed his house to be built on that spot. So a useful compromise! The living quarters of the family are up a flight and the mosaic covers the lower floor. Not only does the householder have his home and fields, but he has a bit of tourist trade for himself enhanced with the picnic tables he built as well.

Walking up another hill in the area, we found the Byzantine mosaic located within a small national park.

Next we backtracked towards Jerusalem to a right turnoff pointing the way to St. George Monastery. But we soon turned off to the left onto a gravel one-lane roadway with hairpin turns going down the mountainside. Ora, our teacher guide, and the bus driver had a short, very verbal discussion about taking the bus down this grade. It seems no bus had ever tried it before! Simply because there were three miles of hairpin curves! But Ora was adamant. She had driven down in a car. It was possible for a car; therefore, by her reasoning, the bus could drive down also. The unhappy bus driver reluctantly started on the downgrade. I looked out the bus window straight down into the deep ravine below. Sometimes the wheels fought for traction. Every so often, the bus driver had to back up once or twice to make a certain sharp curve. The Swedish girl in our group became hysterical and was told in no uncertain terms to shut up and stop the screaming. We were all very relieved when we finally reached a flat section of the road, where the bus then was parked. Every one got out of the bus shaking. From this spot, it was another rough two-mile hike down to the Wadi Kelt. Every now and then, we passed by camouflaged gun positions. By this time, if Ora hadn't pointed them out, we never would have even noticed. At last, just as we were about to collapse from the heat, we heard the welcoming sound of water. Around a bend, behind some more rocks, and there it was--a large pool formed by the Kelt. Directed by Ora, we quickly got into our bathing suits and then ate our lunch sitting in the water. This did two things, cooled us down and restored the water level in our bodies. In this heat, we lose one liter of fluid an hour-- 12 to 15 liters a day! We needed to drink at least a liter an hour. But water is not readily absorbed back into the body unless you eat food to go with it. The surprising thing about this desert trek day was that you did not realize that you were losing all that fluid, because the hot winds evaporated it immediately. Also, all that drinking water vanished before it even reached your kidneys. No need for a "rest stop."

From that pool of clear, cold water, we waded upstream to a minute waterfall with green moss and ferns growing around it.

Such a beautiful, beautiful, welcome sight to our eyes. (Later in Europe, we saw the magnificent waterfalls of Norway and Switzerland, but none of those brought the same sense of wondering gratitude to us that the little Kelt did.) "He leadeth me beside the still waters."

Nobody wanted to leave the pool. I think we stayed there three hours. Finally with much prodding from Ora, we started back up the hot and rocky trail to the bus. Then onto the bus and up the dusty, gravel road to the secondary highway. And another fate-filled decision. We would travel the old, ancient road back to Jericho. In the middle of nowhere, so it seemed to us, Ora had the bus stop. We wearily got out and she led us up over the crest of the hill. There across the deep gorge was the Monastery of St. George clinging to the mountainside. The Roman aqueduct was far below, now on one side, then on the other side of the Kelt. Ora told us to crouch down close to the ground. We sat there in a wind that felt like a blast-furnace, looking at the blue roofs sheltering men who have given their lives to God through the centuries. We knew the answer immediately to the question why did the monks build their monastery on the east side of the mountains!

The five minutes we remained there was long enough. We were glad to get back to the bus. The temperature was 158 degrees as the hot, blasting wind swept by. In spite of all Ora saying every 10 minutes, "Now peopleums, drink, drink," one of the students suffered from heat prostration just after we arrived back at the bus. We poured water over his head and whole body trying to cool his body down. He was so very, very sick that it was frightening. Our bus driver was also slightly unwell because he had remained with the bus instead of going with us to the Wadi. Our enthusiasm for rugged desert regions began to wane rapidly. (In fact, later Lorraine and I gave up our trip to Masada when we learned that the temperature there was equal or above 150!)

Our very first trip to Jericho had been the Saturday after we arrived in Israel. We had gone by Sherut taxi, first to the ruins of Jericho, and then headed back towards the Dead Sea. Once we had to stop to let a herd of wild camels cross the road. Nothing on earth smells as bad as an unwashed camel!

The Dead Sea is a muddy bath of minerals and salt. You couldn't sink if you tried. Our small, wiry, Arab guide helped us, one on either side of him, to keep our balance as we sank into the mud holes under the water. The sea is very medicinal and our legs, especially Lorraine's, were helped. It would have been great to have more time to spend "taking the cure" there.

Once out and showered free from the salt, we dressed and drove down to Qumran. The Essene settlement has been excavated so that you can walk around the site and view the baths, workrooms and cisterns, and imagine how it might have been. Off to the west, you can see the openings in the mountainsides that mark the caves where the scrolls were found. However, you can't go exploring in the caves any more because of the erosion.

The trips from Tantur were much more informative for us than our own attempted excursions. At Tantur we first studied the history of the places we would visit and then our teacher went along with us explaining what to look for and what it meant.

Sometimes though we went exploring on our own. Lorraine and I weren't the only ones to attempt to do something foolish.

Fr. Al Burke, our fellow student and a Maryknoll priest from Japan, decided to walk the Old Roman Road from Tantur to Jericho by himself. Sometimes he walked in the aqueduct itself; sometimes he had to climb up and down the cliffs. Just before reaching the safety of the Monastery of St. George, Fr. Al had a very difficult experience of exhaustion from the heat and the climb. He was very fortunate and made it all of the way through in his venture. But the desert is not a place to trifle with. This was a very unwise stunt, even for an experienced walker like himself.

Yusef Saad, the young Arab who works at Tantur, acted as our guide to Hebron where Abraham is buried. The bus ran smoothly over the 20-mile stretch. Most interesting of all were the grape vines planted in terraces up and down all the wadis in this region. The grapes hang in large clusters, not as enormous as the ones the spies carried out in Joshua's time, but still large enough to brag about. Two men carrying a bunch of grapes is Israel's official tourist insignia.

Hebron has another distinction. It is the oldest continuously occupied unwalled city in the world. Abraham came to Hebron 3,000 years ago and bought the cave of Machpela to bury his wife Sara (Gen. 28:8, 16). Eventually, Abraham, Isaac, Rebecca, Leah and Jacob were buried here also. According to Jewish tradition, this cave was also the grave of Adam and Eve. Now the whole area is covered by a fortress-like structure built by Herod the Great. His trademark, huge building blocks, form the lower walls. Some of these stones are more than 20 feet long. These outer walls of Herod rise to more than 40 feet. But the upper parts of the wall were later additions as the Jewish temple was converted into a Byzantine church in the 4th century, into a mosque in the 7th, then into a Crusader church, and finally into a mosque again by Saladin. Inside the structure, the cenotaphs are huge stone "huts" covered with heavy, richly embroidered drapes. At least they haven't changed as the building that covers them has done over the years.

Once back outside, we explored the village market place and a small shop where a man sat outdoors making tiny oil lamps. We bought a few to bring back with us. So carefully packed were they that not one broke until we were unpacking them at home! On the outskirts we stopped to watch the glass blowers at work. Hebron glass is a distinctive type and comes from one of five factories operated here by the members of one family. The most popular shade is blue with a hint of green.

Back on our way again, we soon turned off to Ramat Al Khaled where we gazed in awe at a gigantic ancient oak supposedly the one near which Abraham pitched his tent when the three angels delivered their message about Sara bearing Isaac. Abraham's Oak isn't quite that old, but is about 600 years old and that covers quite a bit of history. David was also supposed to be anointed king near this site.

Further on, we turned to the right to view three large rectangular pools of water. These are known as Solomon's Pools, although they may have been rebuilt by Herod the Great. Moreover, just across the road opposite Rachel's tomb in Bethlehem, there is a small wall. When we examined it, we found that the inside of the wall was hollow. This little wall is ancient and was once part of a system that conducted water from King Solomon's Pools to Jerusalem over 3,000 years ago.

SECTION I
OFF TO GALILEE!

When the Holy Family returned from Egypt, they went to live in Nazareth of Galilee. On July 1st, a Friday, we were ready to jump aboard our school bus and head for Galilee! It was an 8 a.m. departure from Tantur. Then from Jerusalem we climbed up Mount Scopus headed toward Ramallah. On the way, we passed Sha'afat, the biblical Gibeah. This was Saul's capital when he became the first king of Israel. The ruins show that his "palace" was no more than a prosperous farmhouse for the times. It was Solomon who began the real "kingly" trend of building large structures with forced labor. Speaking of kings, King Hussein has an uncompleted palace here perched on a hilltop, just as it was left when its construction was interrupted by the Six Day War (June 1967).

Previously, Fr. Piccirillo had taken us out to see the Maccabean Tombs. Those stone "hut" affairs are not too interesting to me because once you have seen one, all the rest are look-a-likes. The square structure covering these tombs was perched on the top of a hill and had two trees off to one side, whose shade was welcomed promptly by me. However, most of the students, including Lorraine, climbed up a steep stairway and walked around on the flat roof for a fine view of the surrounding countryside. On that same trip, we also examined the ruins of a water system dating back to Biblical times. Plus we went through the site of Emmaus.

We noted the Arab village of Beitin, which marks the site of historical Bethel--the House of God where Jacob dreamed (Gen. 28:12-18). Winnowing of wheat caught our attention near Shiloh, the religious center of the tribes of Israel before the time of David and the Temple at Jerusalem. Eli and his wayward sons served the Holy Ark and the Tabernacle here.

Back on the road northbound, the mountains of Samaria are higher and rockier than you would imagine them to be. Just before entering Schechem (modern Nablus), we stopped for a drink of cold water from Jacob's Well where Jesus and the Samaritan woman had their conversation (John 4:5-9). The Convent of Jacob's Well is entered by two large metal doors painted a bright blue. Inside there are tiny garden plots. Then two small cement buildings, and two 18-step passageways leading down to a small chapel whose walls are covered with old paintings and icons. Incense burners hang from the ceiling and in the center is Jacob's Well. The well itself is 35 meters deep. We poured some water back into the well and waited a long, long time before the splash. While the topmost structure of the well, about 4 meters in height, is Greek, the rest of the well proper is original stonework from Jacob's day.

The Greek Orthodox priest who minds the well is the lone survivor of a more religious time a hundred years ago, when the Russian Orthodox pilgrims came by the thousands. On the grounds is a huge unfinished church started by the Russians in 1912. This graceful structure made use of an older Byzantine church for part of its outer walls and in the mosaic floors. The work stopped with the First World War. Now the Greek Orthodox Church cares for the Russian Orthodox holy places, but there will never be enough money to finish building this basilica. This unfinished site holds within itself an unfulfilled dream.

Just a hundred yards from Jacob's Well, a small, white, domed structure similar to Rachel's Tomb marks the site of

Joseph's grave here in Schechem (Josh. 25:32). Mount Gerizim stands steep over against Schechem. The Samaritans, though only a few in number now (275), still celebrate the Passover on its summit.

Next, a short 9-mile ride through the fertile valley to the tiny Arab village of Sebastia, where some of the ancient stones from the capital city have been reused in their houses. Here and in other villages also, we saw the young girls carrying large square oil tins full of water on their head to their homes. The older women are barely visible as they are occupied with household chores. The men just seem to sit around in the village squares and smoke, while the young boys buzz around the tourists asking for money and just goof off. Truly the Moslem world is a male chauvinist place. This was brought home to us time after time in the Arab villages in Israel.

Samaria, even as a ruin, shows the foresight and genius of the Omri kings of Israel. The top of the hill provided an easily fortified place, a beautiful view of the surrounding land, and a spot for the cooler breezes to blow. The ruins here are very extensive. The gateway to the ancient capital is flanked by the well-preserved ruins of round towers. The main thoroughfare traversed the city from west to east, with tall columns lining the way. Here are the foundations of the Palace of Omri and Ahab. Excavations have also unearthed many pieces of carved ivory. We, however, contented ourselves with finding potsherds from the period of the Northern Kingdom.

From Samaria, we continued north and then took the left fork at Jenin for the further 16-mile drive to Megiddo. This is our Armageddon of the Apocalypse. This is where legend says the nations will gather to fight the last great battle on earth.

I hope this prophecy will never come true. But this pass has been the scene of many, many historical battles. On the hilltop are the remains of a fortified city. The great stables of King Solomon (10th century B.C.) were located here. There also was a water tunnel; the depth was 60 meters and the length was 120 meters. A path wound down around the sides until the water was reached. All the labor of bringing up this water was most probably done by women. And it looked to me as a very difficult and slippery job.

Back on the bus, completely exhausted from hiking through all these historical sites and climbing over all these hot, rocky ruins, we settled for looking out the windows to see how the modern Israelis were making the desert bloom. The valley has the appearance of the most cultivated, fertile place in all the world. Trees, fields of cotton, and vineyards under rotating sprinklers, cover the land. But it wasn't always this way. The Israelis are merely restoring what the Turks destroyed. The Turks denuded the entire country of trees so the land reverted to its natural semi-desert state. We rolled through 'Afula, the market center of the Jezreel Valley, and on to Nazareth. We dashed through the beautiful Basilica of the Annunciation and were soon in Cana viewing ancient stone jugs like those used in the wedding feast. Onward we sped, to collapse for the night at the Yaalon Hotel in Tiberias. The night was restless, for the trip had been much too much for us, and especially for Lorraine.

(We also felt very frustrated because we had spent such little time in Nazareth. We promised ourselves that we would go back; and so we did after school closed.)

As Jesus spent most of His teaching and preaching time here in Galilee, I now resume the saga of our field trip with the school.

No matter how tired or restless the night, the schedule is always met. It was up and out on Saturday morning, July 2nd. Breakfast was a fast meal at the Yaalon Hotel, and we had to be finished in time for the 8 a.m. departure. The early morning found us on a scenic trip south along the shores of the Sea of Galilee with a stop just before we crossed the Jordan River. For fun, everyone went wading. To keep my sandals dry, I had put them high on the third step of the cement stairway leading into the water. Suddenly a motor boat came racing by making large, splashing waves up even to the top of the stairs. Caught by the waves, my sandals started floating down the Jordan River. I hurriedly waded after them. But before I could rescue my sandals, I was up to my waist in water. My soaking dress clung to me as I got out of the Jordan to put on my sandals. I pulled out my skirt and was flapping the hem, while I wondered how I could sit on this wet fabric on our vinyl bus seats. However, to my surprise, my dress was completely dried by the heat almost before I recrossed the road to get onto the bus.

We drove north along the east shore of the Sea to the Kursi excavations and then turned east to climb up the Golan Heights. Once upon the top, it was easy to see why it was such a strategic place. From the Heights, everything below is like a sitting duck to a hunting soldier. Guns and rusty tanks acted as reminders of the recent war. The descent on the other side via the Yarmuk River Valley is very, very steep. We did not find it too reassuring to realize that specks of sunlight were glancing off the artillery of the Syrian troops across the River Gorge! Hope they knew we were just curious sightseers. Once down the Golan Heights, we retraced our route to Tiberias and headed north along the shore via Magdalor, a fishing village, to visit the scenes of Jesus' active ministry.

About 9 miles from Tiberias, we turned right at Talgha, which means Seven Springs. The Church of the Multiplication of the Loaves and Fishes is a rectangular barn-like structure built to preserve the beautiful ancient mosaics that were the floor of a Byzantine church which once stood on this spot. The mosaic in front of the altar is a basket filled with bread and flanked by a fish on either side. The mosaic floor of the church proper is among the finest to be uncovered in Israel. Even after 1,600 years, the colors are bright and the workmanship superb. Birds and plants of the region are shown, as well as fortresses and a round tower like those used to measure the rise and fall of the sea on the shores of the Nile in Egypt. It was a breathtaking history lesson in itself.

A short distance away was the tiny church of Peter's primacy perched over a rock on the very edge of the Sea of Galilee. This is where the Lord said "Feed my lambs." Medieval pilgrims called this site Mensa Christi, or Table of the Lord.

Only two miles away is ancient Capernaum. The most thrilling part of the trip for me was seeing the tiny house of Peter, which had been converted into a house-church by the very first followers of Jesus. According to ancient tradition, an octagonal Byzantine church had been built over the site of the house of Peter. In the center of this church was a mosaic of a peacock. In the 1960s, this mosaic was in a very bad state of preservation and visitors kept breaking off bits of it. Finally Fr. Virgil Corbo, an archaeologist, was sent to lift the mosaic and to reset it in concrete. While the peacock mosaic was up, the archaeologists decided to look and see what had been under the church. The whole area proved to be covered with the remains of houses dating back to the first century! The most important part was the discovery that the house directly beneath the mosaic had been converted into a house-church. The interior walls had been removed and plastered. The pilgrims of the first century had cut graffiti into the walls calling on Jesus, and the name of Peter was found twice. So this must have been the very house where Jesus cured the mother-in-law of Peter and spent so much time with the apostles in Peter's own home. It also struck me that all these houses (they were not much more than huts really) in the little village were so small and poor. Yet the villagers had built a beautiful synagogue to worship God. The village roofs hardly reached the level of the stone pavement of the synagogue. In contrast to their black basalt houses, the synagogue was constructed of white limestone that would catch the first rays of sunrise and gleam as the sun rose across the lake, or would glow in rosy tint as Peter and the other fishermen came home with their catch of fish. Lorraine stood on the stone quay dock reflecting on the fishermen and their waiting wives. I wandered about looking at the ancient pillars and carvings. I was especially captivated by one of a wagon that might have been a picture of the Holy Ark from the olden days when it was moved from place to place.

The Mount of Beatitudes is only about two and a half miles from Capernaum. A large hospice there is run by the Italian Franciscan Sisters. But we climbed up the hill to eat our lunch under the shade trees at the top. It was so pleasant to sit there overlooking the Sea of Galilee. This was the very same view that Jesus had when he gave his sermon on the mount. The peaceful echoes of Jesus' "Blessed are the poor in spirit, the meek, the peacemakers..." surrounded us in this quiet place. There was a little chapel built about halfway down the hill. It was such a light, fragile affair with slender pillars framing the porch around the central core of the building. Inside, the seven virtues are represented in symbols around the altar. Like a butterfly, it perched among the flowers on the Mount of the Beatitudes.

In the afternoon, our field trip continued through the countryside, past Rosh-Pinna established in 1882 as the first Jewish settlement in Galilee. Its name means "cornerstone" taken from the psalm "The stone which the builders rejected has become the chief cornerstone (Ps. 118:22). Rosh-Pinna is situated at an important crossroads in eastern upper Galilee. The wild wheat that was discovered here has been developed into the strains that are producing in the fields of Israel today.

For five and a half miles, the road climbs north to the site of the biblical Hatzor. Here we examined the rock walls of ruined fortresses, because this had been an important town in the land of Canaan even before the Israelites arrived in the 13th century B.C. Fighting then and fighting now! The Kibbutzim bear evidence of it. The town of Kiryat-Shemona is named in memory of eight young people who died in defense of nearby Tel-Hai. At Tel-Hai there is a statue of Tel-Hai, the lion of Judah, bearing the inscription: "It is good to die for our country" followed by the names of these eight men. Joseph Trumpeldor, whose last words were those on the inscription, was born in Russia, came to Palestine in 1912, and became a leader in the pioneer agricultural movement. Trumpeldor is the Israeli Nathan Hale or George Washington. We stopped at Kibbutz Hagoshrim for dinner and overnight at their guest house. We learned of the history of this Kibbutz, and enjoyed splashing in their swimming pool to cool down.

Breakfast at the Kibbutz with another 8 a.m. departure found us ready for the next adventure. At the Banias River Waterfall, we stopped for our outdoor Eucharist. It felt just like the Lord's Day there beside the rushing water. I think because of one's experiences in this hot, dry land, you really begin to appreciate the value and beauty of water. You can not take water for granted; it is not something to exploit but to treasure.

In the afternoon, we visited Banias (Caesarea Philippi) where the springs form a natural pool, one of the sources of the River Jordan. Herod's son Phillip named the area Caesarea, so eventually it was called Caesarea Philippi. There are shrines and a natural cave here that were devoted to Pan by the Greeks. Now there is a Nature Reserve at Tel Dan. Here we thoroughly enjoyed the lush natural scene, following a twisting, winding path through a wild, untamed place of water and foliage. We explored beneath low-hanging branches, jumped over numerous little creeklets, and just had lots of fun like youngsters.

Back on our road past Kiryat Shmonah, we took a right-hand turnoff to the "Northern Road" which runs west adjacent to the Israel/Lebanon border straight to the Mediterranean Coast. The border itself is about 40 feet wide of barbed wire no man's land. Running next to the Israeli side is a wide dirt road that is examined for marks of infiltration every morning and then raked. The border is a very tense area. Once all of us, including our Arab driver, ducked, and turned white with fear as suddenly out of nowhere two army planes zoomed so close we could see the pilots. Two seconds later they were gone over the mountain crest. Our school bus remained stopped until all us civilians got our breath back. Later we accidentally made a wrong turn and found a border military Kibbutz directing us out of the area in no uncertain terms.

We were scheduled to view the Mediterranean from Rosh Hanikra. But as there had been several border incidents close by, we had to push on down the coast to Akko (Acre, the New Testament Ptolemais). This town is mentioned in the Tell-el-Amarna Letters. It was called Akko then and later by the Greeks and Romans, Ptolemais after Ptolemy II, king of Egypt. The crusaders made this their main seaport and renamed it St. Jean d'Acre after St. John, because the Knights of St. John had their headquarters here. There is a magnificent room known as the hall of St. John which probably served as the dining hall of the Knights. From this hall, we explored part way down a secret passageway that leads to the sea. We found ourselves in another series of Crusader halls. These were originally the hospital quarters of the Knights of St. John.

In this town there are people living in the very same rooms the Crusaders once occupied. The Klan (inn) has been in use for 2,000 years. Its vast courtyard is now part of the noisy, smelly market place.

Back into the bus, we traveled south along the coast. Then in early twilight, we climbed Mt. Carmel to stay at the Stella Carmel Hostel. A lovely couple runs this very Christian place. Their hospitality and kindly atmosphere is well-known and appreciated. But we could have used less spirituality and more practicality in this hospice! The beds were so uncomfortable that Lorraine and I had to pull our mattresses off the beds and onto the floor. There we slept fairly comfortable. But we were mighty glad to see the sunrise!

Up and out again by 8 a.m. Still it did seem in a small way like our own 4th of July, because we drove south along the coast to Caesarea where we had a chance to walk in the sand, and to watch the waves, while we examined an aqueduct. (Beach time without the hot dogs!)

King Herod the Great had founded the city about 22 B.C. and named it in honor of Augustus Caesar. Josephus mentions in his Antiquities how Herod spared nothing in making this a sumptuous place and a safe haven for ships. Caesarea became the capital of the Romans in Palestine for about 500 years. The Byzantine influence lasted until 640 A.D. The walls and fortifications of the city had held the city's enemies at bay until a traitor showed the invading Arabs the famous sewers of Herod. The invaders simply walked through the sewers taking the city by surprise. Later the Crusaders recaptured Caesarea and built defense walls and a dry moat enclosing about 22 acres. Finally the whole city was reduced to a mere heap of ruins by Malik al-Ashraf in 1291.

Nevertheless, even from these scattered remains, one can reconstruct in imagination the greatness of this city. The great high-level aqueduct, under whose arches we walked on the seashore, carried drinking water to Caesarea in pottery pipes. The low-level aqueduct was open on top and carried water for irrigation. Close to the aqueduct, there was once a synagogue, as told by the fragments of mosaics and the marble capitals decorated with seven-branched candelabra and other symbols. Next, we envisioned the crowds pouring into the Hippodrome to watch the horse races. This oval track is 1,056 feet in length and 264 feet wide. Twenty thousand spectators could watch. A square granite pillar about 40 feet long lies stretched out in the grass. Near it are three highly polished blocks. We never did figure out the purpose of the long pillar, but the smaller blocks, in reflecting the sun like mirrors, were used to frighten the horses so that they would bolt.

There is a Byzantine forum of the 5th or 6th century paved with marble slabs and a tri-part gate with two marble pillars in its center. On either side of the gate are two very large headless statues carved in the 2nd and 3rd centuries. The one of red porphyry probably represents Emperor Hadrian. The subject of the white marble statue is unknown. (Fame doesn't last if you lose your head about it, I thought.) North of the gate, a flight of ten steps leads to a higher street that is paved in mosaics.

South of the Crusader wall lies a large Roman amphitheatre. It was built in the second century and shows the development of the theater from then until the Byzantine era. Now in our century, the local authorities have strengthened and renovated the amphitheater for current entertainment. For the first time in 1,700 years it was used in 1961 when Pablo Casals played here. The acoustics are still excellent, we discovered, as we listened to our school leader lecture about the ruins. On the hillside above the amphitheater are many strewn columns, each painted with a number, waiting to be joined together by workmen long gone.

All too quickly, it was time to depart. The bus headed south to Netanya, then took a shortcut to Nablus, and hence to Jerusalem. We arrived back at Tantur, tired, happy, and a little saddle sore from the vinyl seats. Lorraine and I had developed the habit of taking along a pillow, which did help somewhat in this matter.

SECTION II
THE HOLY CITY

The best way to begin to explore Jerusalem is a "Walk on the Walls of the Old City." At least that is what Dr. Walter Wagner, the Director of Tantur, thought. On our first school afternoon, Monday June 27th, he led the way up onto the ancient soldiers' walkway on top of Jerusalem's Walls. It was a very rugged walk and had us hugging the wall and inching along in spots. Often your foot would slip on the worn stones. There were many great views of the city, but I did not glimpse many of them. I was just plain too busy hanging on to the wall and watching my footing to let my eyes go gazing about. Birkenstock sandals are not the best footwear for this type of uneven slippery walking. It was a tense two and a half hours to circle the city. But I made it, I am proud and happy to say. (Lucky I didn't break my neck or at least twist an ankle.)

That evening, it was much more relaxing to sit in an easy chair listening to Dr. Richard Cleave's tapes and slides. Dr. Cleave is a medical doctor who became more and more interested in finding a way for those who could not travel to the Holy Land to make a spiritual journey to this Holy Land. His photography is excellent and his tapes are inspiring and spiritually moving. Later, on Monday evening the 18th of July, Lorraine and I had again the rare treat to visit Dr. Cleave and have him show us his workshop. He lives for his work in a rambling old house not too far from the White Sisters. Afterwards, we walked back to the sisters through the empty streets under the stars thinking of how life was then at the time of Christ.

What was Jerusalem, itself, like in the olden days? The archaeological excavations near the Temple Mount have helped trace the historical process of settlements close to the vital heart of the city. There a young girl guide made the whole historical story vividly alive for us as she punctuated her remarks leaping like a mountain goat upon the huge stones that the Romans had toppled from the Herodian wall to the paved street below. Years after the Roman destruction, during the early Byzantine era, Christian inhabitants renovated and constructed homes in the area. Then during the Omayyad period, from being a residential quarter, the area changed back again into public buildings. Thus each succeeding group left its mark in the ruins before us.

Outside the Holyland Hotel, there is a large outdoor model that represents Ancient Jerusalem in 66 CE, (Common Era) just before the beginning of the First Revolt against Rome. The sources used were the Mishnah, the Tosephtha, the Talmud, Josephus and the New Testament. Its scale is 1:50 (1/2 inch = one foot). Original materials of marble, stone, wood, copper and iron were used. The present excavations are showing even more insights about these buildings of old Jerusalem.

Besides exploring the Temple Mount, we also walked around the ruins of the City of David on another hot afternoon. Then we decided to check out King Hezekiah's tunnel built to carry water into the city in case of siege. We went down to the spring and waded knee-deep through the cool waters into King Hezekiah's tunnel. At first, we started out barefoot. I quickly decided that I would rather not have my feet in ribbons from the sharp pebbles, and put back on my trusty sandals. So for some 1,800 feet, with the rock walls high on either side of us, we stumbled along in the dark until we came out into the light at the Pool of Siloam. The workmen had started from both ends of the proposed tunnel. In spite of the twists and turns, the crews finally met in the middle within a yard or two of each other. Now that is remarkable!

Across the valley is the tree-studded Hill of Evil Counsel. The palaces of the Sanhedrin were situated here. (name coincidence?) Another day, we traveled a different road from Bethlehem to Jerusalem just to stop and look at the splendid views of the city. An interesting sidelight is that from this road you can see caves in the opposite hillside that have been inhabited for centuries! I would have liked to be able to find out from the present day dwellers how they are managing. The limestone slopes, the pine groves, the sheep grazing and Bedouin with donkeys, take you back in imagination to the pastoral lands of Biblical times.

Another road that offers an excellent view of Jerusalem is the road to Jericho just past Bethany. The pilgrims from the wilderness of Judea must have stopped abruptly and sang in their hearts as the Mount of Olives and Mt. Scopus appeared, with the little village of Bethany to their right. Now we remember this village only because Jesus raised Lazarus from the dead there.

The Franciscan Church of St. Lazarus, built in 1954, suggests by its very architectural lines a funeral chapel. The gray color of the walls and the sculpture of two angels pointing out the empty tomb of Lazarus accentuate this. In contrast, though, the resurrection is promised in four mosaics: Jesus with the friendly family of Bethany, Jesus promising the resurrection, Jesus calling forth Lazarus, and Jesus at the supper given by

Simon the Leper. However, a mosque covers the actual site of Lazarus' tomb. Therefore, you have to walk around the mosque and in by a side door. Then you go down a few steps to some shelf graves in a small cave.

Using the appropriate scripture readings, our class walked together over the stony hillsides to reenact Palm Sunday. Jerusalem has three main gates into the city: Damascus Gate (across the street from where we stayed with the Sisters), Jaffa Gate (full of bullet holes from the Six-Day War), and the Lion's Gate (also called St. Stephen's Gate) just opposite the Garden of Gethsemane. In all, there are eight gates in the old fortress-wall. The inside of Jerusalem itself is divided into five sections: the Christian Quarter, the Armenian Quarter, the Jewish Quarter, the Temple of Mount (Mount Moriah), and the Moslem Quarter. (Our little Arab guide on one of our individual outings decided to take us back by a shortcut through this Moslem section with its blue doors representing a pilgrimage to Mecca. A rock got into my sandal, so I stopped to shake it out. This meant that I fell a bit behind Lorraine and our guide. And thus found to my surprise a few rocks bouncing off me! This was the first time in my life I was ever stoned! For the moment, I was stunned. Then I quickly took to my heels, and caught up fast to the guide and Lorraine. They had been so busy talking that they had not even noticed my dilemma. That gave me inside as strange a feeling as the actual stoning.)

The easiest way to the Temple Mount is through the Jaffa Gate across the courtyard and down the few steps into David Street. David Street changes its name to Chain Street but ends at the Wailing Wall. On the maps, it is shown as a straight, wide thoroughfare. Maybe so, but we found that the width is very much cut down by shops extending their wares into the street, the teeming mob of people, the pushcarts, the overpowering smells, the archways blotting out the sky, plus a maze of twists and turns.

Finally, we broke through the crowds into an open space to view the Western Wall (Wailing, because of the loss of the Temple.) The Israeli have dug down ten feet at the base of the Wall to expose the stones that date from the Temple built in Herod's time. Lorraine and I went up to the Wall on the women's side, and offered our prayers for peace.

Then we climbed the staircase to the right of the Wall into the Temple Mount area. This part is still guarded by Jordanian soldiers, as it is a Moslem holy place. Before we were finished visiting these various sections, we just automatically opened our purses and bags to allow the various soldiers to peer inside for guns without even conscious thought.

The El Aksa Mosque is the first shrine with its silver dome. You leave your shoes at the door and enter a broad open hall. The floor is covered with Oriental rugs. No furniture, just rows of marble pillars in Byzantine design. It is possible that this was originally the basilica built in honor of Mary by Justinian in 536 A.D. In the front part of the mosque, there are the burnt remains of a wooden pulpit set on fire by some insane person.

Outside to the right of El Aska Mosque is a small door leading to an underground area called Solomon's Stables. This large section housed Roman and Crusader horses, as well as Solomon's, tethered to its large pillars.

The southeastern corner of the wall on top of Solomon's Stables is called the Pinnacle. Here Satan tempted Jesus to cast himself down. It is quite a fall to the ravine below. You would suffer much more than a mere "dashing your foot against a stone."

The Temple Mount itself is a stone-paved platform about 30 acres in area. Heading toward the Dome of the Rock, we watched Moslems washing their hands at a fountain called El-As. It is equipped with a circular row of pink marble seats, each with a faucet in front. Passing the fountain, we went up a flight of steps and under a Roman arch called, in Arabic, Almizan or "the Balances." Popular tradition has it that on the Day of Judgment a pair of giant scales will be suspended from these arches and our merits and demerits weighed.

The Babylonians in 587 B.C. had destroyed Solomon's magnificent Temple. The second temple was built around 520 B.C. Herod enlarged and beautified this temple which was the one that Christ called His Father's house and that was so prominent in the New Testament. In turn, this temple was destroyed by the Romans in 70 A.D. when they reduced Jerusalem to rubble.

The present mosque on Temple Mount was erected in 691 A.D. It is called the Dome of the Rock because it was built to enshrine the rock that tradition holds to be the place upon which Abraham was to have sacrificed his son, Isaac. The rock itself is about 30 feet by 30 feet. This same rock was held to mark the center of the earth, as everyone in those days believed the earth to be round and flat. Therefore, the Jews call it Even Hasheteya--the Stone of Foundation. On medieval maps, Jerusalem was always placed in the center of the world. In addition, Mohammed was to have ascended to heaven from here.

The Mosque of Omar (Dome of the Rock) is an eight-sided building faced with marble slabs and multicolored mosaics. Around the outside of the building, quotations from the Koran are written in Arabic script. The golden colored dome is supported inside by pillars which encircled the rock itself. The marble used here is striped gray and streaked purple. Red plush carpets cover the entire floor. Stained glass windows in the dome filter the light. Also there is a cave-like chamber under the rock where the souls of the dead are believed to assemble for their prayers.

The Dome of the Rock is surely one of the most beautiful structures in the world. Nearby stands a very small building which is almost a miniature of the Dome of the Rock. Some people think it may have been the architect's model. At any rate, it is called the Dome of the Chain.

On Thursday, July 7th, all of us students set out to retrace the events of Holy Thursday evening. Up Mount Zion, we went on our devotional walk. Finally, we reached a medieval structure of two stories. Going into its small courtyard, we sat or leaned against the pillars for a talk and scripture reading. A cave beneath this building was discovered about 1158 A.D. This is believed to be the resting place of King David. Quietly, we entered the small tomb room containing the stone cenotaph of David with the silver crowns of the Torah. This tomb of King David is one of the most revered of the Holy Places in the State of Israel. This tomb cave, along with the words of Peter in Acts 2:29, gives credence to the tradition that the dining room of the Last Supper was over the tomb of David. After praying there, we then climbed the outside stairs on the side of the building over the tomb.

Reaching the structure's upper room, we found a large hall with pillars and decorative arches. A mosque is occupying one corner of the room and a few steps lead to two small rooms opposite. This could easily be the large Upper Room, "well appointed," where Jesus and His disciples ate the Passover together before He instituted the Holy Eucharist. This space is just an empty room now, but it could easily have accommodated Jesus, the twelve apostles, and the women who cooked the Passover.

Afterwards, Jesus and His disciples walked down into the valley and crossed the Kidron to pray in the Garden of Gethsemane. Gethsemane is a corruption of the Hebrew name Gath-Shamma, which means Oil-press. The eight ancient trees here are shoots sprung from the roots of the original trees under which Jesus prayed. These olive trees, old and gnarled, probably looked the same as those that witnessed His sorrow that night.

The Basilica of the Agony next to the garden of Gethsemane is called the Church of All Nations because each of its 12 domes were donated by a different nation. The front of the church is decorated with a large colored mosaic depicting Our Lord suffering along with the poor, unfortunate people of the world.

As we entered this Basilica, we could feel the anguish and sorrow. The interior resembles a dark and starry night. Light filters through the blue and purple windows, dimly lighting the way to the Rock of the Agony in front of the altar. The Rock itself is surrounded by a low grill of bronze representing thorns and olive leaves combined. Midway, on three sides of the fence, are birds drinking from a cup representing the cup of pain from which Jesus asked to be freed. On the two front corners of the grill are large silver doves caught in the thorns, representing Jesus as an innocent victim. The ceiling of the church consists of 12 domes filled with mosaics. These have various symbols dealing with the Passion and Death of Our Savior. Especially prominent in each dome are mosaics of ancient olive trees with their branches reaching upwards.

The original church next to Gethsemane was built in the fourth century. This present one preserves much of the original design. There are three apses, as also was in the original, and the floor is a reproduction. Even the ancient water channel is marked by a zigzag black and white marble strip. The 12 pillars in the Basilica are of the rose colored limestone known as Bethlehem marble and are capped by marble capitals, again copies of the original. Everything this architect, Antonia Barluzzi, has done serves to make this a place of shadows, a place of meditation, and a place of prayer.

A short distance further down the hill is an ancient grotto where, according to tradition, Jesus left eight of the Apostles and where, when he returned, Judas betrayed him. There are three altars in this cave with paintings of Jesus with the Eleven, the betrayal by Judas, and the last, the Assumption of Our Lady.

From Gethsemane, we crossed over the Kidron and walked up the ancient steps that once were the main street in the southern section of Jerusalem in the time of Christ. Up these very stairs, Jesus was pushed and dragged as a common criminal to the House of Caiphas by the soldiers on Holy Thursday night. These are the very same rocks Jesus had often trod on his way to the Temple. Walking up this stone stairway, I experienced a deep sense of reality. To me this was a heartfelt feeling that I was actually walking after Jesus. This seemed much more important to me than my mere emotions when gazing at a painting depicting a scene in Jesus's life.

Over the courtyard where Peter wept, the early Christians built the Basilica of Saint Peter at the House of Caiphas. Later the Crusaders added the name of "Gallicantus" (the Cockcrow). The present church was built in 1931 after the site had been excavated. The main mosaic in the upper church represents Jesus in the Judgment Hall. The mosaics on either side depict well-known men and women of the time who were sinners. (If it were to be painted today, whose faces would be on the billboard?)

The most heartrending part of this visit was to descend to the lower underground prison where Jesus was kept. The prisoners were lowered by ropes under their arms into a very deep hole. From a window high above, a guard stood watching from within the scourging room. There is a step cut into the rock so that the eye can reach the spy-hole, which is quite high.

In the scourging room proper, there are two rings in the upper rim of the rock between two pillars. The actual scourging pillar, which has been removed, would be exactly in between the two pillars and beneath these two rings. On one side is a stone couch cut into the wall for the bleeding prisoner to rest. This is an absolutely authentic site and gives one a very realistic picture of what happened to Jesus that night and to other prisoners as well. It was quite a brutal place of torture.

Underneath the Convent of the Sisters of Zion in Jerusalem is a first-century stone pavement. Because of the markings in these stones, they are believed to be part of the Fortress Antonio. That place then would be where Jesus was mocked by the Roman soldiers. The Ecce Homo Arch stands just outside. Nearby is the Franciscan Church of the Flagellation. Here the domed ceiling above the altar is a Crown of Thorns. As the thorn branches reach upward towards the center, they turn into a blossoming tree. This symbol caught at our hearts especially after we had just seen the prison. Immediately, we prayed for all those in prison unjustly. Fr. Michele Piscirillo also showed us later his work with grave stones and toured us through the Flagellation Museum.

When we made the Via Dolorosa with the class, it was difficult not to get lost in the crowded streets. In fact, three of us did so. The Swedish girl, one man, and myself arrived at the Holy Sepulchre with none of the other students in sight. It was my opinion that we ought to stay together, and wait at the church. Our teachers knew the city and our destination was the Holy Sepulchre. However, the lone male of our little group thought the "rest" were lost so, therefore, he should go back and find them. I walked with him a bit until my common sense reasserted itself. Why was I following along with this man when he was no more acquainted with the streets of Jerusalem than I was? We would both be lost. Therefore, I turned back at the Church of the Redeemer, which I explored for a while.

By the time I returned to the Holy Sepulchre, I found our Swedish classmate hotly arguing with the Israeli guard. She was wearing a sundress with bare shoulders. We had been warned about our clothing at the school, because reverence in dress is taken very seriously here. She ungraciously refused an offer by the guard of a scarf for her bare shoulders and stalked off in a huff. This left me standing alone in front of this huge shrine that covers Calvary. Holy Sepulchre actually is many churches in one, each with its own traditions and its own ownership of space. Quite a jumble! Just inside the doors is a marble slab marking where Jesus was anointed.

When the whole class finally arrived, we entered to visit the various sites within. Lorraine joined me and we climbed up the stairs on the right to the silver ornate altars of the Nailing to the Cross, the Crucifixion, and the Sorrowful Mother. There is a hole beneath the altar so that you can touch the Holy Ground. No souvenirs allowed! Yet, we obtained many! It happened in this manner. As a class, we had gone underneath the present shrines to where workers were now doing much renovating. When a workman passed by us hauling a wheelbarrow full of dirt and rocks from the Hill, Lorraine asked politely for some of his rocks. Thus, we had our authentic relics! It was also interesting, while walking beneath the church, to watch a stonecutter painstakingly chip a design into a marble slab just as it was done in the ancient times.

Back on the main floor, the Greeks have built a high wall around their portion of the Basilica. This is a shame because the wall cuts off most of the main church and gives one a boxed-in feeling. In the beginning, this was originally the choir section of the Crusader Church. Around the outside of this wall are various chapels. There is a fragment of red granite believed to be part of the Scourging Pillar to be found in the Blessed Sacrament chapel. Therefore, we attended Mass there.

The most special center of it all is, of course, the Tomb itself. I thought it very strange that the Grave would be standing in the middle of an open space. But the explanation is quite simple. Constantine, in his zeal, had the hillside cut away, leaving just the bare earthen walls of the Tomb in the center of the vast church. In its original state, this Tomb, like all such Jewish tombs, consisted of two rooms. In the inner one would be a single burial niche in a side wall. After the body placed here had been reduced to bones, these bones were then placed in a stone ossuary in the outer room. That meant the niche was then ready for the next user. If a death occurred before the first niche was vacated, another niche would be carved out.

In 1810, the Greeks built the present outer shrine over the Tomb. This first part is called the Angel's Chapel. The marble table here contains a stone set into it that is believed to be a piece of the original stone that had closed the tomb. A low doorway leads into the actual burial chamber. Milling crowds of pilgrims were moving constantly in and out of the tiny tomb. I had a real dilemma. Upon leaving home, a friend had pressed a bottle of olive oil into my hand. She wanted that particular bottle of olive oil to be blessed at the Tomb. It was a miracle that I was able to carry the oil this far without breaking the bottle. It would take another major miracle to get that oil blessed with the constant flow of people in and out of the tomb. But when I turned around and looked at the tomb again, there was no one there! I entered all alone, and I gave the oil into the hands of the Greek monk. While the monk was uttering his lengthy blessing for the oil, I knelt in silent prayer with my hands resting on the Tomb of Our Lord. Not a single person entered the tomb until after the blessing was finished and I had left the tomb. No sooner had I cleared the doorway, though, the crowds poured back in. The Lord had answered my friend's prayer completely. I was amazed at what had happened. It certainly wasn't logical.

Back of the Tomb itself, the Egyptian Coptics have a tiny, poor, little shrine which we visited. However, the monk there gave each of us a wooden cross with a grave smile and a blessing. This so touched Lorraine that she emptied our purse for him. Nearby, against the earthen wall, were many other graves showing that this whole area had been a burial spot in ancient times.

To have a realistic idea of the actual natural setting of the Tomb in Jesus' time, it is well to visit a completely different site. Back of the Arab Bus Station is a rugged hill that, due to excavations, resembles a skull. In 1882, General Gordon became convinced that this was the real Golgotha and so it is now called Gordon's Calvary. There is a typical tomb of the first century there. The grave is surrounded by a garden so that one can pray and rest quietly thinking of the Lord. This sends one away with a peaceful heart.

SECTION III
MODERN MEMORIES

The whole country of Israel does have very special qualities about it. Truly, it is a Holy Land. Yet it is a Sad Land also--there is evidence of painful memories, of suffering, and of poverty. And probably, there is still more trouble to come for this special place.

On Sunday, July 10, we had another of our famous field trips. The usual 8 a.m. departure. This time we went to the Hadassah Hebrew University Medical Center. It is an enormous plant; 1,000 patients and 750 personnel doing mainly research. They had so many visitors --300 a day-- that an information center, faced with Jerusalem stone, was built to explain the work of the hospital. It was named after our President Kennedy. We watched a film there showing a typical day from start to finish at the hospital, which is a specialized training school. Next, we stood in awe before the beautiful stained-glass windows in the hospital's synagogue. Chagall has depicted in abstract terms the Twelve Tribes of Israel. These precious windows were removed for safety during the war. The hospital, itself, was damaged during the Wars of 1948, 1967, and 1968, but not during the war in 1973.

Painful memories are recalled in the Yad V'Shem Memorial. We were definitely sobered by the exhibit of photographs and effects relating to the slaughter of the Jews by the Nazis. The "Holocaust" is captured within a structure of mammoth, uncut boulders. The entrance gate is an anguished, agonizing pattern of shapes. Inside this stone memorial flickers a flame by whose light you can read the names of Bergen-Belsen,

Auschwitz, Dachau...engraved on floor plaques. I remembered the pitiful pictures that a returning soldier friend had taken of the walking skeletons that were the only survivors of Dachau. No wonder the Israelis have nightmares of their past sorrows returning to them.

At Tantur, we had talks to acquaint us somewhat about the complex problems of today. Mr. Farah Al-Araj, former mayor of Beit Jala, discussed the "Concerns of West Bank Palestinian Arabs" on the night of July 8th. On Sunday, July 10, we had a Jewish-Christian Dialogue led by Dr. Geoffrey Wigoder. We came quickly to the conclusion that, as Americans, we had absolutely no idea whatsoever of the complexity of the problems faced here by both the Jews and Arabs. We cannot even imagine the stress on the individuals and on the country.

Nevertheless, it was good to have these few insights into modern problems because we had had so much "Archaeological Updating." Dr. David Noel Freedman, about whom we knew from S.F.T.S., gave us students an evening session at the Albright Institute on the "Ebla Tablets" on July 5th. Ora Lipschitz, between her lectures and field trips, had filled us in on the Conquest Narratives and the sites of Jericho and Ai.

On another field trip, this one led by Dennis Young, we admired the Knesset. This is a magnificent structure of peach-colored stone housing the Parliament. The Israeli claim that the Israel National Museum is the largest between Rome and Tokyo. It has four main components: the Bezalel Art Museum, the Samuel Bronfman Biblical and Archaeological Museum, the Billy Rose Garden of Sculpture, and the Shrine of the Book. We didn't even begin to see all that we wanted to see in the Biblical and Archaeological Museum. The architecture of the Shrine of the Book is outstanding. The curving top resembles the jar covers in which the Dead Sea Scrolls were discovered. Here are the Scrolls, letters of Bar Kochba, and special finds from Masada. This building gleams with its 275,000 glazed white bricks. Nearby stands a decorative black marble structure, so that one cannot fail to grasp the contrast between the Sons of Light and the Sons of Darkness!

At another time we also visited the L.A. Mayer Memorial Institute for Islamic Art. Arabic script has artistic beauty within itself.

We did have our lighter moments as well. The evening of July 6 was spent at the Jerusalem Khan for an Israeli Folklore program. That was one of our "Big Splurges." The Khan was first a Turkish caravanserai. Now, after many changes of fortune, it is a place for lively Israeli dances and folksongs. A large group of touring Jewish youngsters from America was there the same night we were. All of us were caught up in the music and dancing. We felt a sense of belonging.

On a different level was the Pop-Musical, based on the Book of Ruth, we attended in the ballroom of the Jerusalem Hilton. Here in ultra sophisticated surroundings, the simple story of friendship and love was told. "Your People are Mine" started at 9 p.m. and kept us highly entertained on the evening of Saturday, July 9, for two hours.

Then the Sunday before we left Tantur, July 10, we enjoyed an evening meal followed by dessert and coffee in the Monks' Quarters because it was the Eve of St. Benedict's Day. That, too, was a pleasant, stimulating time.

All too soon it was time for our Farewell to Tantur. Of course, we had a party, plus time for summary and evaluation discussions. Another great schooling experience in our lives was closing. We were so very grateful for our chance to be at this unique, wonderful school. It was hard to admit the session was over, and that we had to "go forth" using our enriched knowledge and memories.

SECTION IV
BACK TO THE FRANCISCAN SISTERS

Back to Jerusalem and the Franciscan Sisters we went on Friday, July 15th. At first, we were housed on the lower floor of the main building, but on Monday we were changed to rooms in a little Retreat House used by the Sisters near their outside gate. This small building contained a tiny oratory with a beautiful little tabernacle for our visits and prayers. Two of the Franciscan Sisters and the two of us were accommodated on the upper floor of this retreat house. This gave us a feeling of privacy and of being on our own.

On Sunday we walked about three miles hither and yon, trying to find a 10 a.m. Roman Catholic Mass in this Holy City with hundreds of churches, not to mention the thousands of priests and religious. We kept being directed to one church after another, but one had had their last Mass at eight; another at seven; and so it went. Finally, we walked back to the White Sisters. With fresh directions, we set out for the Dominican 'ecole Bibloque. Supposedly there was an 11 a.m. Mass there, but nothing happened until 11:30. It was to be an ordinary low Mass. However, we cannot be positive about this for the Mass we attended was sung in French and concelebrated by 11 Dominican priests! If this was ordinary, I wonder what they would do to celebrate a big feast day?

Tuesday, the 19th, was an extra special day. I started writing my journal at 4:30 in the morning. Yes, that's right "in the morning." The sun was already up. It seems to rise about 3 or 3:30 a.m. The day held the promise of another hot one. After breakfast, Lorraine and I took #75 Arab bus to the village of E-Tur, where the Mount of Olive Road begins to wind downward. Since this is a very steep hill, we were very wise in choosing to walk down rather than up. (We are learning!) From the right hand side of the road, we often paused in awe at the spectacular views of Jerusalem on the hill opposite. But where was the place of the Ascension that we came to see? There was an imposing building near our bus stop. However, this proved to be a boys' school. One of the youngsters deigned to show us to the correct spot. He pointed to a gate and a bell. We rang. This time it was a Russian Monastery. The monks kindly gave us further directions. We walked on passing a man with a camel. "Did we want our pictures taken on a camel?", he asked. Although he assured us repeatedly that the camel had had a bath, it still wasn't hard to say "No, thanks." (Didn't use DIAL or LIFEBUOY soap on that camel.)

Finally, we arrived at the Ascension site. The Crusaders had built just a plain wall around the spot. This, with its open courtyard to the sky, was as powerful a symbol as anyone could wish for. Unfortunately, the Moslems placed a small Mosque exactly in the middle of the yard. This was a plain, poor looking specimen, not even worthy of the great Arabian architecture. Enough said.

Back on the crest road again, we passed the Carmelite Convent and paid a visit to the Church of the Pater Noster, where we read the Lord's Prayer in 44 languages on the tiles.

Again, we started down the hill and immediately came to the Tomb of the Prophets. We enjoyed talking to the caretaker very much, who showed us his tiny garden plot. Moreover, he was also a very good guide. He took us underground to the burial places of Haggai, Malachi, Zechariah and 49 of their disciple-prophets. The whole thing was hewn out of solid rock in a horseshoe shape. The outer curve of the horseshoe had the tombs cut into the rock. We walked around center passageway of this horseshoe and then found that within the curved inner wall, there was a tiny space for an inner oratory. Hard to explain, but if you draw it you have a horseshoe within a horseshoe. (Now who would be interested in something like that but me?)

Once out of the cold underground tombs, we said goodbye to the elderly caretaker and continued on down the hill. The entire left side of this mountain is covered with Jewish graves, both ancient and modern. It is a very sacred place indeed to the Jews. Also the Moslems have their graves from the valley floor up to Jerusalem's Walls on the other side.

We took a right-hand path to the modern "teardrop" church. This "Dominus Flevit" chapel marks the spot where Jesus wept over Jerusalem. As we looked out, we saw, framed by the window, the Temple Mount and the Dome of the Rock shining in the sun. Back to the main road again and this time we met a man with a donkey who offered us a ride. But the poor little donkey had a sore foot, so we quickly refused.

Next, we glimpsed the Russian Orthodox Church of Mary Magdalene with its onion-shaped spires through the trees. It was built in 1888. This could only mean that Russian Orthodox Sisters would be close by. I had a special personal quest that I wanted to fulfill on this journey down the hill of the Ascension. While working at Point Reyes in California, I had become friends with Abbess Julianna, a Russian Orthodox Sister. She had confided to me many events of her life in Russia during the persecution. Also, Abbess Julianna had spoken so fondly of her friend, Abbess Barbara who had suffered together with her in a Russian prison. After release, Abbess Julianna and a few sisters had then come to America. Abbess Barbara had gone to Israel. Our director at school had told me that Abbess Barbara was a recluse and never saw anyone. Nevertheless, I wanted to see and talk with Abbess Barbara and I figured God would provide a way.

Just before we joined the main road again after leaving this beautiful Orthodox church, a car drove up and parked. The driver started unloading his car and handing out long, leafy stalks to a Russian Orthodox Sister who was working on the pathway. I went up to this sister and told her that I had known Abbess Julianna in America. Would it be possible for us to talk with Abbess Barbara? Sister lead us up their pathway to a small convent to wait in a very old-fashioned parlor. Along the path was a group of young novices stripping leaves off the branches the man had brought. We never did discover what cooking secrets were being prepared. Finally, after a 45 minute wait, we went downstairs to the inner hermitage of Abbess Barbara. She, who was usually bedridden, had been helped into a chair to receive us. This dear friend of Abbess Julianna was in her late, late 80s, or 90s, but still had a keen mind and spoke English well. She reminisced about the "old days" and I told her how I came to know Abbess Julianna and of her death. Abbess Barbara then told us to pray and spoke of her fears that we may have a nuclear war. Certainly we were surprised to hear such a logical insight from someone so old and so spiritual. We asked for and received a blessing from this very holy woman.

Our very special visit being over, we continued on our pilgrimage past the Garden of Gethsemane and the Basilica of the Agony. Near the foot of the hill, we descended down 47 steps in semi-darkness into St. Mary's, an underground church. At the bottom, we turned right to where, according to ancient tradition, Mary was buried. Also there are two side-chapels, one for Joachim and Anne; the other for Joseph. This day on the Mount of Olives had been a very full pilgrimage, and so filled with spiritual, emotional, and physical happenings that we were exhausted. Prudently, we caught a bus to return to our hospice.

The following days, from the 20th to the 22nd, were our adventure time via Sherut taxi to Nazareth and Tabor.

On Wednesday the 20th of July, we got up at the early hour of 3:30 a.m. to catch a Sherut taxi outside our door at the Franciscan Sisters at 4 a.m. Our driver also doubled as a newspaper carrier. As we sped along, (he did drive very fast) he dropped off bundles of newspapers and picked up more passengers. The Arab passengers were friendly, but it is hard to discuss politics with a limited vocabulary of "yes", "no" and "thank you." We arrived at Nazareth just in time for the special 6:30 a.m. Mass for religious in the lower Basilica with the altar in front of the Grotto of the Annunciation.

The Basilica is one of the loveliest churches we have ever seen, truly a joyful mystery. The architect, Giovanni Muzio, has very sucessfully preserved the remains of all the previous churches: the house-church of the first century, the Byzantine Basilica of the 4th or 5th century, and the Crusader Basilica of the 12th and 13th centuries, in this completely modern structure. From Casa Nova Street, you enter a small, open plaza and find yourself in front of an imposing cream-colored limestone church. Several vertical bands of rose limestone break up any monotony that might result from the one color tone. There is a statue of "Jesus the Teacher" above and then a relief of the Annunciation cut into the stone below. The great entrance doors are of bronze and copper with scenes from the life of Christ. To the left in the vestibule are the 12 Old Testament prophets cut into red marble, and on the right are the 12 Apostles.

But instead of going in at this point, visitors usually walk around the building to the right and enter a doorway on the south side. The doors here consist of 12 panels portraying the events in the life of Mary. As soon as we entered the south door, we saw a large octagonal opening surrounded by a bronze rail. We could actually look down into the old Grotto, or what is left of Mary's house against the further side, where the angel appeared to her. Behind the Grotto is a portion of the wall of the Crusader Church. In front are several pillars and mosaic work from the Byzantine Basilica. The baptismal font dates to the first century. When we received Holy Communion, we walked down the short flight of steps into this section. What a very special blessing this was for us!

Afterwards we looked at the five beautiful Crusader capitals from the twelfth century at a side altar and the six mosaic panels commemorating the visit of Pope Paul VI to the Holy Land in 1964.

Then we ascended one of the great spiral staircases to the upper church. This part is used as a parish church and also has a large opening in the floor to view the holy Grotto below. The side walls are covered with panels called National

Banners. These are either mosaics or ceramic pictures of Our Lady. In the one from Japan, the white in Our Lady's shawl is composed of hundreds of tiny cultured pearls. It is breathtaking! Looking up to the ceiling, the dome of this church seems to me to resemble a lily. A fitting tribute to Mary!

Going out the north doors, we found ourselves in a large courtyard. Here stood a clear glass structure that took us a while to realize that it was a modern Baptistery. We are not quite up on the ultra, ultra modern as yet. In the yard itself there are many relics, including columns and Crusader Capitals. Just past the monastery is the Church of St. Joseph built over the site of Joseph's carpenter shop. There are also viewing sections here showing how the homes and shops looked at the time of the Holy Family living in Nazareth.

After this beautiful start in the early morning, we started off to find the Sisters of St. Charles Borromea's Hospice where we would have breakfast, rest, sightsee, and spend the next two nights. Unfortunately, we turned to the right instead of to the left. We walked and walked. The sun rose higher and higher in the sky. Helpful passersby told us to climb up and up. It grew warmer and warmer. Finally, we collapsed on the doorstep of the Franciscan Sisters at the top of the mountain (same order as we were staying with in Jerusalem). When they took one look at us, they understood our situation. Very kindly, they brought both food and water. Then after dishes, one sister, who was going shopping, escorted us half way down the mountainside and gave us exact instructions to the Sisters of St. Charles. What an exhausting experience!

Strange to say, we were the only guests at this hospice of seven beds. Perhaps, because it was so small, people just assumed it would be full, like all the bigger places. These were Sisters from Germany, grown old in their years at Nazareth. The "young one" of their order was 64. All the ones we met were well, well over 70 at the very least! However, they served us delicious meals in beautiful style and were so very hospitable to us. We certainly admired these sisters for their many kind deeds. When we reach their point in life, may we be as gracious and good to those we meet.

After we recovered a bit from our long morning hike up the hill, we walked back to the Annunciation Church and spent a few hours there lost in contemplating its beauty. We also stopped and heard a Mass at the Greek Catholic Church on the way. Mary's Well is the most authentic spot in Nazareth. It has been the only well in the town since the very beginning!

Unfortunately for enjoying a peaceful spiritual atmosphere, Casa Nova Street springs into action with hundreds of street peddlers every time a tour bus is due. These hawkers and so-called guides of the Holy Places are a very disturbing distraction. I'd like to use the old word "disedification." At any rate, they are really more like the flies swarming over the spiritual banquet offered to the earnest pilgrim!

In the main section of Nazareth, we arranged for a taxi to take us to Mount Tabor on the next day, Thursday the 21st. While there at the stand, we learned of and later met an elderly lady who actually was walking from Jerusalem to Nazareth and the other Holy Places. That kind of pilgrim we will never be! Our feet and legs have swollen from the heat. Our muscles have been very sore. Gradually they have firmed and strengthened from all our walking and climbing. Our sandals have been a Godsend for us. They make our feet so happy! Still our hikes have to be in the one-digit range for us to survive. And not all uphill at that!

We invited the Sisters of St. Charles Borromea to come to Tabor with us. The last time two of them had been there was 20 years ago. (That's just like we are. We do not visit places close to us until a visitor comes by and would like to see the interesting spots.) Mount Tabor is a one hour drive from Nazareth. This hill sits by itself in the middle of the plain and it is 1,994 feet straight up! The road twists and turns to climb the steep incline. No bus will undertake the drive. You either walk straight up for three hours or take a taxi. That was the reason our school bus stopped at the base of the Mount, and told us to gaze at Tabor from the valley below. I'm glad we now made our own trip, for the rugged ride up the mountain was all that it was claimed for it. This isolated mountain is a most fitting place for the Transfiguration of Jesus. To see more of the view of the countryside, we climbed up onto the roof porch of the church on the right-hand side. Then we climbed over the cement slabs on the left to drink in another glorious view. That was really Tabor to us! The church itself was also striking. Back of the altar was a large semicircular stained glass window on which was embossed two resplendent peacocks. The mosaics also of the Transfiguration were beautiful. As we entered, a Mass was in progress. We stayed for it and for the next Mass also which, to our surprise, was a pilgrim Mass for the 45 Belgian Sisters whom we had met at the Franciscans only yesterday. Their Community had sent them on this pilgrimage together. We were a bit envious. Maybe we could promote the idea of a group of our sisters traveling together to visit the Holy Land. What a great idea for Community Building! On our pleasant ride back to Nazareth, our driver even stopped his taxi so we could examine the yellow blooms on the cotton plants in the fields along the road.

Still ready for adventure, in late afternoon we climbed back up the hill to the Salesian Basilica of Jesus the Adolescent. It is a lovely gothic structure with white marble reaching straight up to heaven. The pillars are really different. They are made up of a cluster of very slight columns rising straight up to the vault without any capital. A white marble statue of Christ, carved by Bogino, overlooks the sanctuary. To get in the church, however, we had to arouse one of the monks. He didn't mind being disturbed from his work and also gave us a tour of the Salesian School there. Over 400 boys attend. While the thrust of the curriculum is vocational, the youngsters have eight years of study with four languages: Arabic, Hebrew, English, and French. And we, ignorant Americans, only know one language!

Then down winding lanes to find the little old church of the Mensa Christi. It was erected in 1861 and all it contains, really, is a huge, somewhat flat rock that legend claims Jesus and His Apostles dined there after the Resurrection. Whoever dreamed up that idea, surely didn't use his imagination. It would have been better to claim that Jesus and His boyhood friends in Nazareth sometimes played at the rock "Zealots and Romans," their version of "cops and robbers." However, who is logical? This church, as it is, is not even a minor tourist attraction. We had to spend quite some time locating the elderly lady who had the key to the church door.

Next, we visited the modern Maronite Catholic Church that had a nice fresco of the Angel and Mary back of the altar.

While most tourists don't wander down back alleyways, we thought we could save time by taking a shortcut through the Jewish section of Nazareth. Suddenly, stones began to be thrown at us! Why?, we wondered, as we walked quite a bit faster. Now Arabs, Moslems, and Jews have pelted us with rocks. Are we equal opportunity targets? While at school, we didn't have the slightest idea that such fear? such bitterness? existed. Our teachers always included both Arabs and Jews. Face to face, people seemed friendly enough. Certainly, such intense hostile feelings toward mere strangers walking by cannot bring good tidings for the future, in my opinion. Hope and pray that I am wrong.

It was good to sit outside at the Sisters of St. Charles Borromea after a delicious meal, just to relax from the day, and look at the twinkling lights of Nazareth.

The morning of Friday the 22nd, we attended Mass at the huge Carmelite Monastery next door. Here 17 Sisters pray for the welfare of the Holy Land. After yesterday, I think their prayers are needed. Above their altar is a statue group of the Holy Family with a painted picture of Bethlehem in the background. We said some very special prayers here for our family at home and for this Land.

Back at the hospice, Lorraine and I made up our beds with fresh bedding for the next guests. The sisters were much surprised. They had not realized that we, after years of convent life, could very easily figure out "their" traditional system of where they had put the linens away. Back to the White Sisters we returned, happy that we had really seen Nazareth.

Upon our return to Jerusalem, we walked around the outside of the walls via King David Road until we were directly beneath the Dormition Monastery. We glanced at the suburb to our right named after Sir Moses Montefiore. The sight of a windmill gave us a start. But this strange windmill has had quite a history. Its original purpose was to be just a plain, old windmill grinding grain but then it got caught up in the war for independence. Today it is a museum. Then we crossed the road and, rashly, decided to climb straight up the steep slope of Mount Zion. Such a shortcut I never want to take again. Almost at the top, our way was blocked by a rock wall. Lorraine managed to climb over it. Even with her tugging and pulling, I almost didn't make it over the wall. So much for being a mountain goat in Jerusalem! I would rather be a sheep in the level fields.

Dormition Abbey was erected in 1906. In the ceiling is a golden mosaic containing a picture of Mary with the Infant Jesus. The most striking part of the church is a huge circular inset in the floor containing the signs of the Zodiac, the names of prophets and saints, plus the symbol of the Holy Trinity in the center.

We had tried again and again to see St. Ann's Church and finally succeeded on our last day in the Holy City. Then outside of St. Ann's, we walked around the ruins of the pool of Bethsaida. Examining the ruins, you could understand the words "five porches." The fifth one was in the middle.

Finally we had seen all we came to see, and much more besides. This called for a celebration with a delicious glass of fresh Israeli orange juice.

In a way, it was a shame that now, after we really knew our way around, we had to head for home. Practically, we decided to lighten our baggage a little. We took our infamous, troublesome box, jammed it full, and lugged it up Jaffa Road to the post office sending it home with our rock souvenirs and school notes. The White Sisters accepted graciously all the "medicines for sick tourists," which we had really never needed to pack in the first place. Once again we looked at the bullet holes and the "wear and tear" of war in the closed Notre Dame de France. Again, we thought of the beautiful statue of the Virgin holding the Infant Jesus in her arms on the hillside in Abu Ghosh. As we relaxed in our room, we laughed over the Turkish Bath that our Arab guide had shown us. Harem imaginings are not for active women of today's world.

We crowned our night at the Tower of David with a Sound and Light Show illustrating Jerusalem's troubled history. It was a beautiful and moving experience. We walked back to the Sisters along the Walls from the Jaffa Gate to the Damascus Gate under the stars without a fear, for Jerusalem is fundamentally a very safe city.

Our flight to Athens was scheduled for 5:50 a.m. from the Lod Airport on the morning of July 27. As Jerusalem is about 40 miles from Tel Aviv, we thought to leave Jerusalem on the 26th and have an easy night at the airport hotel in preparation for the flight. This was a ghastly mistake. However, it had seemed a very reasonable plan back in California. What was wrong with this idea would soon unfold to our dismay.

Tuesday, July 26, was our "day getting ready for the flight." We made plans to meet Niole (a French professor with whom Lorraine had made friends in Jerusalem) in Paris.

Remembering our train experiences in Spain, I thought she had better have our hotel address just in case. After all, six countries and six weeks stretched between now and France. Niole was, however, positive she would be there to greet us as we got off the train in Paris. Our goodbyes were said to the Sisters and we hopped into our Sherut taxi by 8:35 in the morning. Our driver was a little early, so we had a totally different tour of the outlying sections of Jerusalem as he picked up his four other passengers. One was a young man who spent the whole time giving practical advice to his younger companion. Whether she was his sister or his girl friend, we could not decide. The morning ride through the Jerusalem Hills with pine trees planted on the rocky slopes was very pleasant. Already, in our hearts, we were missing the Holy City.

The airport was reached in good time and we checked most of our luggage. Next we tried to locate our Avia Hotel or the hotel bus. It had simply disappeared. Where was this hotel that supposedly was at the airport? Finally, a #495 bus was pointed out to us and we were crammed aboard with a hundred more or less other squashed people. The driver did not comprehend our situation. However, the friendly passengers tried to help. Out into the flat, hot countryside, we went. Finally, some one spotted a sign "Avia Hotel" and shouted out. The bus jerked to a sudden halt and we were deposited in a cloud of dust on the roadside. The bus rattled off. We looked around. Acres and acres of dead sunflowers surrounded us as far as our eyes could reach. Near at hand was a herd of munching cows. A two-car lane threaded its way toward a distant modern structure. Could this be our "Mecca?" Resigned to our fate, we trudged down the road hot and tired. It did turn out to be the elusive Avia, Israel's Aviation Hotel. But near the airport it was not!

We registered, asked to have a taxi call for us (certainly there would be no buses at 3 a.m.), and were shown to a pleasant room overlooking the courtyard and a swimming pool. The first thing to do was to cool off and rest. As the afternoon wore on, activity and noise kept increasing outside our windows. Waiters were busy setting up for an outside banquet, plus a band. How could we sleep through that! The problem was easily solved. In a twinkling, we were moved to the room across the hall. Another complication! The door to the balcony wouldn't open. We were locked in without air! The hotel's handyman fussed with the lock and then gave up, saying the lock was too complicated to fix. He would have an assistant help tomorrow. Meanwhile, he would push the window open a bit for us. After he left, Lorraine climbed through this tiny space and opened the balcony shutters. We rested and gazed over the dry field, this time filled with grazing sheep. So this day turned out to be a day of rest rather than a sightseeing venture to Tel-Aviv after a quick check-in at the "airport hotel." Dinner was excellent, with turkey steak, tender and juicy, as one only can get in Israel. Then we went peacefully to sleep to await our taxi call.

Suddenly, I woke with a start. I looked at the clock. The front desk hadn't called us. Even worse, they had not ordered a taxi! Finally, one was located and we were on our way by 3:30 a.m. At long last, we were checking in at the terminal. The search at the airport was very thorough. The girl asked who packed the suitcases and I told her that I did. She lifted

LUCILLE HINTZE

everything out very carefully and put everything back very carefully so that all fit, which was quite a feat. She asked if anyone gave us anything. We chorused "No" thinking of the cost of every item! The body search, they eliminated. We must not have looked the "spy type." Then into the plane and off for Athens at 5:50 a.m. with the many happy memories of the Land that Jesus loved and cherished in our minds.

CHAPTER VI
THE GLORY OF ATHENS

TWA made our morning with a scrumptious breakfast of scrambled eggs and mushrooms. By the time we were finished eating, the plane was landing on the golden shores of Greece. Airport buses are quick transportation and soon we were in the heart of Athens. A short walk and there we were, in our hotel, unpacking. Our room had a balcony giving us a view of the Acropolis, which was especially spectacular at night with the lights on the marble ruins. We were very pleased with our 382 drachmas ($11.58) Hotel Acadimos. (Another plus for Arthur's Book!)

No bus for us! We stretched our legs and walked on our own sightseeing tour back to Syntagma (Constitution) Square. We paid a short visit to St. Denis the Aeropogate Catholic Cathedral. Within the church was a shrine to Our Lady of Lourdes. Many people, who had been ill, had asked Our Lady to plead with her son, Jesus, in their behalf. When their illnesses were cured, they wanted to show their gratitude in some manner. Therefore, they decorated the shrine with hundreds of bracelets and jewels of all kinds. It looked a little too much! I thought maybe they ought to start a soup kitchen or something else in thanksgiving instead of decorating. More practical. Or maybe to the cured, only jewelry would have a sentimental value. However, who am I to judge their feelings of gratitude?

Just past the Parliament buildings, we stopped dead, completely fascinated by the honor guards at the Tomb of the Unknown Soldier. They wore white cotton tights, a short brown skirt over white ruffles, a black jacket with red trim. Their heavy wooden shoes sported black pompoms. As we watched, we noted that practically every tourist around wanted his or her picture snapped standing right next to the guards. These honor guards did not move a muscle, but one of them showed by his eye movements how much he disliked the whole affair. Finally, we tore ourselves away from the sight of honor guards and their outfits, and had a stroll through the National Gardens. Just as we came out of the Gardens by the gate of the ex-king's palace (now used by the prime minister), two black limousines sped down the driveway into the main street with two soldiers stopping the oncoming traffic. More honor guards stepped away from their tiny pill box guard houses and snapped to a special salute for the occupants of the limousines. Speeding Fame! These particular guard houses had canopies, of all things! We went back again into the Gardens, roaming around until we reached an open space containing the massive ruins of the Temple of Zeus and Hadrian's Arch. These massive pillars were at least five stories high.

On the way back to our hotel, being hungry, we went into a family restaurant. They didn't understand us nor did we understand Greek. Nevertheless, we took a chance, pointed at some strange Greek words on the menu, and found, to our happy surprise, we had half a delicious chicken with a tomato and rolls to divide. We kept the waiter busy bringing us cold water to drink. The weather here was much cooler than in Israel but, unfortunately, much more humid.

Once we had rested and bathed back at the hotel, we found we were again ready and eager to take the afternoon bus to the Acropolis.

A wide gravel-paved road leads upward to the Acropolis. The sweeping views of the city and countryside caused us to pause several times as we began to realize how the ancient Greeks enhanced their innate sense of beauty. That huge platform on top of the hill had more marble per inch than any other spot in the world, I imagine. It must have been breathtaking when the devotees streamed through the huge foregates, past the six caryatids (six women holding up a roof with their heads) and into the Parthenon. It would make even the dullest devotee look up with renewed devotion.

The Acropolis museum itself is sunk deep into the ground so that it will not disturb the regal silhouette of the temples on the Acropolis. The museum contains many of the artifacts. We found the huge statues and carvings very realistic. One, that was especially lifelike, was of a lion grasping an ox in his jaws. There was also one of a war scene that transported you into the midst of battle.

There was so much to see and wonder about that we stayed on top of the Acropolis until they announced closing time. Before leaving the hilltop, we took one last look over the Plaka, or the oldest quarter of the city. We admired the ancient Agora (market place) and the theater of Dionysius on the south slope as we went down the hill. We had followed in the footsteps of St. Paul and that night the Acropolis, bathed in golden light with its altar to the Unknown God, looked down upon us mortals fast asleep.

Should such "seasoned travelers" as we take a "tourist Greek Island tour?" Oh, no! We confidently took the subway on Thursday to the seaport of Piraeus, carrying our little picnic lunch. The fruits here, especially the peaches, are large, juicy and delicious. In fact, all the foods are fantastic and the pastries most delectable. Best of all, the prices are reasonable. Lorraine did note that clothing is mainly imported. The same standard brands are the world over. By the time it took me to write that, we were at this bustling seaport. A trip to a Greek isle is a must. Oh dear, the prices were out of sight for us! It was $150 for this trip and $85 for that one. So we continued to walk along the piers, passing by the bigger ships and their higher prices, until we came to a small ferry. Here was just the right trip for our pocketbooks! We boarded, paid our 33 drachmas (11 cents), and launched out into the unknown waters.

We landed on a small island, which we thought was Salamis. If so, the two other islands across the sea with their barren hillsides and houses clustered close to the water's edge were Aegina and Methana. Next to the landing dock was a dusty bus into which we climbed. As we rode, we saw just the perfect picnic spot. But we were prudent this time. To make sure of the return route of the bus, we rode to the end of the line and then back to the spot we had selected.

We sat on the bank under a long-needled pine tree with the clear blue waters lapping in and out at our feet. Opening our picnic lunch, we feasted both our bodies and our eyes. For a while, families with their little ones were splashing about in the water. We watched a Greek Orthodox monk teach his little boy to swim. Then everything became very quiet as everyone went home for the siesta hour. The blue waters and the blue sky above cradled us in peacefulness. A poignant memory to be stored for the busy, restless years to come. How we hated to bestir ourselves to leave this serene spot. But finally in late afternoon, up the embankment we climbed, took the bus back to the ferry, and to the seaport. Still spellbound, we rode the subway to Athens beyond our Omnia Square stop. However, in retracing our steps, we found another cafe where the price was right. Try "Monssaka," a baked meat dish covered with vegetables. Delicious! Each country seems to have their own very special dishes that make you think you are partaking in a heavenly banquet.

At the National Archaeological Museum on Friday, we saw the fabulous gold "death mask of Agamemnon" plus tiny masks for the royal babies. Two bronze statues had been recovered from the sea near Piraeus where we were yesterday; one was a large running horse with a tiny jockey astride his back; the other was of Poseidon perfectly balanced upon the heel of one foot and on the toes of the other. The ancient Greeks excelled in both sculpture and architecture.

It was our last morning in Athens. Before we left, we walked out onto our balcony and had our final gaze at the Acropolis. Lorraine left a red rose and a "thank you" note for the maid. Such polite, friendly, honest people here! We would like to return.

The airport was a confused mass of people. Being a bit early, the agent pushed us ahead for the earlier flight. Fill out this... Fill out that... Check out... Search? (no time)... Rush up to Passport Control... Rush down to Gate 1... Lorraine was somewhat ahead of me in line. However, by the time the flight attendant herded Lucille (that's me) and the crowd of other passengers into the waiting plane, Lorraine had vanished! The stewardess had to forcefully restrain me from jumping off the TWA plane. I definitely did not want to land in Rome without my fellow traveler. Finally a bus dashed up reuniting friends. Where had the "Lost One" been? Oh, spending the leftover drachmas on postcards, of course. I almost lost my "cool." But all had ended well, so we relaxed. And the plane joyfully winged its flight towards Rome.

CHAPTER VII
THE ETERNAL CITY OF ROME

On the way into the city on the airport bus, we passed a wedding party climbing into an old-fashioned open carriage. The couple looked so festive with all the flowers and the ribbon-bedecked horse. May the bride and groom always be as happy as they are this day, we thought. The airport bus deposited everyone at the terminal and we then took a streetcar to St. Peter's. We trundled our cart after us over the cobblestones as we looked for our Soure Sacre Famiglia hospice. The street, on which the hospice was located, was supposed to be exactly opposite the Vatican Museum. We could not find the place no matter how we tried. Finally, having received similar advice from different strangers, we jumped, bag and baggage, onto a tourist bus driving through the Papal Gardens toward the Sistine Chapel. However, once on the bus we then had trouble convincing the tour guide that we wanted to go into the Vatican Museum with our luggage, and not just ride back with them to St. Peter's Square. Finally exasperated by these crazy tourists, as they thought us to be, they practically threw us into the building, locking the Museum door after us.

Realizing we were now in the back door of the Museum, we dusted ourselves off, checked to see if all our luggage was still with us on the cart, and then merrily bumped our way down the long spiral staircase and out into the street. Once across the street, we met a young woman with a baby and her husband. They were a Syrian couple, who turned out to be also staying at Sacre Famiglia. The only English words the husband knew were "sleep" and "church" but still he would always be telling us something long and complicated and include those two words in it. They accompanied us to hospice and introduced us to the Sister in charge of the visitors.

Sister Angela spoke some English, but she had a sense of humor that could be understood in any language. She made us feel right at home and showed us our tiny twin-bedded room with a large balcony. We unpacked happy to have found our abode in Rome where we were to spend the next six nights. Lorraine fixed us a light supper and we gratefully settled down to rest and renew for the strenuous sightseeing we intended to do on the morrow.

The next day, Sunday, we attended Mass at St. Peter's. In fact, we spent the whole day at the Vatican and really saw only a tiny bit of the treasures there. To approach St. Peter's, we had to cross the Piazza San Pietro. Interestingly, this is not an accident but done deliberately by Bernini, who designed this immense piazza to be a part of the whole experience of St. Peter's. It is an introduction to the Basilica itself. Bernini had several problems to solve: one was to design a space that could accommodate half a million people without detracting in any way from the monumental impression of the church itself. He did this by enclosing the space with a colonnade-- two slim porticos supported by 284 columns. This makes the piazza seem smaller! There are four parallel arms of columns in each arm of the colonnade. The two major arms are laid out along the circumference of an ellipse. When you stand on one of the two foci points, the colonnade nearest you seems to have only one row of columns. But when you look behind you, the other has columns in apparent disorder! The final effect is a tension between reason (what you see ahead) and faith (what you can't see, but imagine behind you). Bernini seems to have had in mind man's perplexity, the visible need for the answer provided by the great church standing in front.

Another amazing feat of Bernini is in the pavement of the square. It looks level but isn't. No matter how huge and compact the crowd in the piazza, Bernini has designed an experience of viewing St. Peter's for each individual in that mass of humanity. We found how high and large this building was when we rode the elevator to the Dome. Once on the roof, we discovered that the seemingly tiny statues of Christ and the Apostles were in reality 18 foot statues looming above us. We leaned over the balustrade and saw people like ants in the square below. Then we followed the upward curving passageways in the largest of the five Domes. Once on the first level, we looked down from the dizzy height upon the marble statues and the mosaic floor below. The magnificent paintings stretched upwards all around us. There was another narrow staircase to climb inside the walls to another viewing level several stories higher. That venture was not for us, we decided! The Dome of St. Peter's is practically as high as the tallest Egyptian pyramid.

The inside of St. Peter's defies description. Its size is enormous, yet everything is perfectly balanced. Huge statues are everywhere. The chapels are filled with art treasures: paintings, mosaics, and sculptures. One of the most beautiful is the "Pieta" of Michelangelo who sculpted it in 1499 before he was 25 years old. The high altar, created from a single block of Greek marble taken from the Forum of Nerva, stands over the tomb of St. Peter. The Baldachino over the high altar is 95 feet high and made of cast bronze. The heavy material has been molded into intricate weavings of branches and laurels, tassels and scrolls. One tiny section would be enough for a cathedral in our country to be filled with joyful sightseers.

Beneath the church proper is the world of the dead. Here in the Vatican Grottoes are to be found remains from pre-Christian to the present. We were impressed by the simplicity of Pope John XXIII's tomb and the array of garden flowers brought by those who simply love him. This church is a living masterpiece by Bernini and Michelangelo, plus many other great artists.

The collections in the Vatican museums and galleries are among the greatest in the world. We could recognize Fra Angelico, Leonardo da Vinci, and Raphael among the hundreds of paintings. The collection of ancient sculptures is the largest in the world. There is a colossal Hercules, the largest bronze statue ever found, and two of the most famous of all pieces of classical sculpture: the Laocoon, father and two sons writhing in a death grip of marble serpents, and the incomparable Apollo Belvedere (400 B.C.). The Borgia Rooms contain a lavish display of the frescoes and paintings of the Italian painter, Pinturicchio. Raphael did the walls and ceilings of four large rooms that overwhelm you with their color and beauty. Pope Julius II was responsible for recognizing Raphael's talent, as well as that of Michelangelo's and Bramante's.

But the Sistine Chapel is the climax. When we finally arrived in this room, it was wall-to-wall people. Lorraine found a seat for me, then one for herself, and we waited for the crowd to thin a bit. Michelangelo's Creation and Last Judgment strike awe into the heart of every individual who spends a moment or two in contemplation here.

Our first busy day was nearing an end. Looking at the time, we realized that, in truth, we had spent this entire day at the Vatican, and that we had really only seen a fraction of the treasures there. We then bought some Vatican stamps to mail letters to our family and friends, and went down those "spiral stairs" for a second time to the street below.

As we were feeling the pangs of hunger, we looked for a nearby restaurant. Unfortunately, the charming one we found with its outdoor tables did not live up to its appearance in regards to the food. We were afflicted quite quickly. Back in our rooms, we felt very miserable. Indigestion, plus fatigue, brought on homesickness and dampened our spirits considerably!

Hearing voices outside, we looked out over our balcony to the walkway below. Sister Angela was working in the garden and chatting with a tall, husky man of middle age. She introduced us then to our future "Guardian Angel in Rome." Youssef Khasko was an exile from Palestine and by trade a composer of symphonies. It was he who had written the English letter for Sister confirming our reservations at the Sucre Sacre Famiglia. Youssef offered to take us sightseeing that very night. As we hesitated, he immediately included the Syrian family who at that moment came through our doors to visit us. So we, four adults plus two-year old Susanna, packed into his little car for an interesting quickie tour of Rome. It was pouring rain as we circled the Trevi Fountain. But Lorraine, bravely, jumped out anyway and threw coins in the fountain to ensure our return. (A tourist superstition encouraged by guides and fountain cleaners?) It is an enormous 18th century wall fountain leaning against the Palace of the Dukes of Poli.

At the center, in the niche, is a statue representing the Ocean standing on a seashell pulled by sea horses.

Our spirits were much recovered by the time we turned in for the night. Unfortunately for me, my stomach was not. Monday night, Youssef drove the two of us out to the lake near Castelo Gandolfo and there treated us to a most luxurious banquet. Everything was out of this world and Lorraine, who was able to eat, said that she had never ever eaten anything like the delicious unborn pig they served. (I was a bit jealous at the sight of all that luscious food and wallowed in a lot of self pity! Oh, how I wished I could have eaten some of that good food.) However, the full moon shining on the dark lake added a beauty and charm to this night that we will long remember.

When Youssef learned of our scurrying about to see the sights, plus our unfortunate eating experience, he shared his knowledge of Rome with us. In the evenings, he helped us plan and told us what buses to take. He also showed Lorraine the market where, before 10 a.m., she could buy fruit, bread, and cheese for our breakfast and supper. Also Youssef told us of the La Madonella, a workman's restaurant, where we could eat very well and inexpensively for dinner. It was so inconspicuous one could pass it by very easily without noticing. However, very interesting and delicious meals were served once you pushed past the beads that formed the screen door. I say "interesting" because in this family-owned restaurant no one spoke English. As we neither spoke nor read Italian, we had no idea whatsoever what we were ordering. We quickly learned never to order the same thing and to trade portions. There was always something to chuckle about. The soup we thought we ordered turned out to be cheese balls; the dessert, a salad. Finally, the owner motioned for us to follow him into the kitchen where his wife was cooking and for us to point out the food we would like! His youngster cleared the dishes and filled our water glasses. The price would be figured on the paper tablecloth, which was then gathered up, and a clean new square put down for the next customer. We enjoyed our simple, nourishing meals there.

Rome was so vast and we tried so hard to take in all the sights. There are churches on every corner in Rome--even twin churches facing each other. Youssef said "Slow down. You'll never visit all the 2,006 churches in Rome!" Actually, I think there is, by count, around 400 if you don't include all the chapels. Well, we did make a fair start on them. Some were magnificent, some were medium. Some were famous, and some were not!

The Cathedral of Rome and the Mother Church of Christianity is the Basilica of St. John Lateran. The houses of the Laterani family, plus the nearby military barracks, were given to Pope Melchiades by the Emperor Constantine in 313 A.D. The earliest church erected here suffered damage from the Vandals and from earthquake. It was reconstructed by Pope Sergius III in the 10th century and dedicated to Sts. John the Baptist and John the Evangelist. It was destroyed by fire twice and rebuilt. In the niches of the massive pillars are large baroque statues of the Apostles by the pupils of Bernini. The ceiling is richly designed with symbols of the church, the Passion and the Coat of Arms of the Popes: Pius IV, Pius V and Pius VI. The upper walls contain scenes from both the Old Testament and the New Testament.

Another church that impressed us was the Basilica of St. Paul Outside the Walls. This is the largest church in Rome after St. Peter's. Some of the meetings of Vatican II were held here. It is historically one of the four major churches erected by Constantine around 314 A.D. The outside facade has on it these large mosaics: Christ with St. Peter and St. Paul, Agnus Dei, and the Four Prophets. The Basilica contains five naves divided by 80 granite columns. Above the columns, running around the center nave, are mosaic likenesses of the popes, beginning with St. Peter. Between the windows are modern frescoes depicting the life of St. Paul.

Santa Maria Maggiore is another vast, but well-proportioned basilica church. Most notable here were the mosaics depicting the life of Mary. The one in back of the main altar is the culminating point of all the mosaics for it commemorates the declaration at the Council of Ephesus (5th century) that the Virgin Mary was the Mother of God (Theotokos). Mary is seated on the throne with her Son. An interesting sidelight here is that the ceiling is gilded with the first gold brought from America by Columbus!

Tuesday, we rode the buses out to St. Callisto's Catacombs on the Appian Way. Brother John, a young Seminarian, guided us through the Catacombs, pointing out the various markings and symbols painted on the walls. We were impressed with the frescoes, faint with age, of Baptism, Penance, and the Eucharist. There is nothing morbid about these early graves of martyrs. However, we were still glad to be up and back into the bright sunshine of a summer day again.

The Capuchin Church that Youssef took us to on our last evening was a totally different story. Here was a famous or an infamous collection. An artistic monk, who had a rather grim sense of humor, used the bones of his long dead fellow monks to fashion fabulous decorations on the walls and ceilings-- thousands of dried bones formed various decorations and flowers. (We decided promptly to be cremated!)

Wednesday, we caught the crowded bus to Castel Gandolfo, about 20 miles outside Rome. Alighting from the bus, we walked up the roadway and finally found ourselves in the front row, no less, in the outer piazza. Pope Paul VI spoke first to the crowd jammed into the smaller inner square and then to us in the outer town square, which was packed for the length of a whole small city block. The Holy Father addressed us in five languages, then waved and smiled directly down on the two of us. (There are advantages of being in the front row.)

After the Pope's blessing, we decided to walk to the plain little village church for a prayer. Then we strolled down the path toward the lake and ate our lunch, sitting on a low stone wall under the shady trees. It was a quiet and peaceful interlude.

But then in mid afternoon, we had to retrace our steps to the bus stop for our return to Rome. It was crowded with milling people. More and more and more persons gathered, as the wait stretched into three hours on a hot Italian summer afternoon. No bus would stop for us, and the mood of the mob grew hostile. Finally one lone bus did stop. We were literally thrown on in the mad rush forward. Suddenly the bus was wall-to-wall people! No one would get off, so the bus driver tried to manage his vastly overloaded vehicle down the road to the outer walls of Rome. There, this mass of squashed and stepped-on humanity was disgorged onto the street!

This ride and being tossed off a streetcar were the worst things that happened to us in Rome. (For the streetcar fare, there was one particular coin you put in the collection box which we had been doing every day. So far, so good. However, one night the fare was changed. This we had no way of knowing; therefore, I had put the wrong coin in the box on the following morning. The conductor shouted at us angrily in Italian and threw us off the bus!) We did very well, usually.

No tour bus for us. We saw the Coliseum, the Roman Forum, other ruins, the Tiber River, the churches, the fountains, the staircases, all by city bus. We had a wonderful time seeing all that was to be seen. And even more! One very amusing thing kept happening. If we went sightseeing without our veils, the hawkers tried to sell us lots of trinkets. If we wore our veils, the hawkers tried to sell us rosaries and medals!

People-watching on the Via Veneto, as we drank a cup of coffee with Youssef, was an eye-opener. Then out into the countryside we went with Youssef for a 45 minute drive to the Gardens of Villa d'Este. The palace grounds are famous for their fountains. Cardinal d'Este built his palace in the 16th century. The grounds opened at 8:30 p.m. and we walked into a spectacular fairyland with beautifully lighted fountains, waterfalls, and other water displays. For more than three hours we walked entranced in these magnificent grounds. What a way to spend our last night in Rome!

However, it was after midnight when we started packing for our morning trip to Assisi. Daylight came all too quickly. (We still haven't learned our lesson completely as yet about midnight packing. Every time it happens we vow we will NOT do this again. When will we ever learn?)

We said farewell to little Sister Angela with her sense of humor and gave her our "Palestinian hats" as a remembrance. Youssef loaded us, bag and baggage, into his car and drove us to the train. There he helped us get a seat reservation and then to find the right car and the correct seat. It was so, so hard to say goodbye. Rome had treated us very well. We had seen all that we had come to see. We had been thrilled to note that the Swiss Guards at the Vatican were still tall and strikingly good-looking in their colorful red, yellow, and blue outfits designed by Michelangelo. We could forgive them for wearing plain, blue uniforms on ordinary days. We had gazed at the fallen grandeur that was once Rome's. We had prayed in countless churches. We had gazed in awe at the genius of Michelangelo. But most of all we knew that we would miss Youssef Khasko who had been a true Joseph to us in the eternal city of Rome.

LUCILLE HINTZE

CHAPTER VIII
MORE ITALIAN ADVENTURES

We were decidedly nervous, as we sat in our reserved seats on Train #2866 at 10 a.m. on that Friday, August 5th. This was our first use of the Eurail pass. However, we made our connections successfully at Orte. Two lively young girls and their father, who were also going to the land of St. Francis, now shared our compartment on the train. The girls were very excited about their trip to Assisi, the home of the gentle St. Francis. Everyone's enthusiasm grew as we realized the next train stop would be Assisi.

From the train station the auto-bus took us all to Assisi which was perched on the green rolling slopes of the hills of Umbria. We were deposited in the center square of the town, bag and baggage. And welcomed by a torrential downpour! Our fellow travelers hurried to their hotels. Lorraine and I scuttled inside the darkened church of St. Clare as the thunder roared in our ears. We wanted to see the church before going to our Guest House. Still, we didn't feel comfortable about leaving our baggage unattended in the back of the church. Therefore, we took turns. While I guarded our suitcases, Sister Lorraine visited the tomb of St. Clare with her preserved body in a glass casket and looked at all the ancient vestments and habits of the first Franciscans. Then I leisurely explored the church.

By the time we had finished, the church was closing for the noon siesta. Walking outside, we discovered the downpour had turned into a gentle rain. Therefore, we were able to carry our suitcases up the winding road across the street from the Basilica without a problem. Up some stairs to our right and soon we were knocking at the door of St. Anthony's Guest House. Dropping our suitcases in our room, we dashed to the dining room in time for the second serving of lunch. A young couple from Canada sat across from us and immediately we fell into a conversation about Assisi. As all of us were to be there for only one day, we were discussing how to explore all of the haunts of St. Francis in one afternoon. Accepting the advice of an older lady traveler from England, we hurried back down to the square to hire a taxi. The young wife did the dickering, as she was the only one of us who could speak even two words of Italian. Finally, the bargain was struck with the driver and we piled into the taxi.

Up into the hills, the driver took us to the Hermitage of St. Francis, 4.51 km. away. We had thought that the rain would spoil our visit to Assisi, but instead it proved a blessing. First off, it forced us to take a taxi which then delivered us fresh to enjoy exploring these sites, and second, the rain enhanced the spirituality of the Hermitage. None of us will ever forget the ethereal beauty of the sun shining through the mist and glistening on the raindrops hanging like jewels from the trees. As we, each in our own personal solitude, walked along these wooded pathways on Francis' mountainside, a sense of beauty and an inner peace stole over us. Such feelings are experienced only on rare and precious moments. We were fortunate on this particular day. Nothing seems to capture the heart and mind of a person as does Assisi. A certain spirit of holiness breathes among the hills of St. Francis. It tugs at you: Come and rest your heart awhile. Let gentle Love enfold you.

At St. Damien's (1.51 km. away) the young Seminarian guide retold the story of Francis and Clare. What courage they had to leave the comfortable homes of their parents to begin a life dedicated to the love of God and the poor! Another 3 km. found us entering the Church of St. Mary of Rivotorto within which the tiny hut, where Francis wrote his "Rules," is preserved. Francis loved and breathed poverty. Then we drove along the valley floor for 4.5 km. to the Basilica of St. Mary of the Angels. This huge church is built over the little church of the Portiuncula, the cradle of the whole order of Franciscans. It is truly amazing that a world wide group of men and women would have grown from such a small, insignificant beginning. Especially since Franciscans embrace poverty as their identifying characteristic! Finally our taxi driver sped back to Assisi for us to enter the Basilica of St. Francis. This is really two churches, one on top of the other. The walls are completely covered with frescoes painted by the members of the Italian Schools of Art of the 13th and 14th centuries. We looked at each of them in turn reading the stories told in the paintings. As we left the church to go back to our St. Anthony's Guest House, we exclaimed, "What a rich and fulfilling day this has been!"

After a peaceful night's sleep, we returned again to St. Francis' Basilica in the early morning. I have the feeling that St. Francis would not have approved of building this Basilica. It is too huge and richly adorned for Francis' taste. At least in my opinion.

Upon our returning to the Guest House, we found a street fair going on in full force back at St. Anthony's. This was a lively change of pace for us. Therefore, we browsed and looked, and looked some more, and finally, bought a small canteen for water.

Then it was time for a quick packing job, and a bus ride to the railway station. Guess who helped us onto our correct train? None other than an elderly, kind Franciscan named Joseph. Another Joseph to our rescue!

This was a very short journey, 12:42 - 3:32 p.m. Before we knew it, our train was pulling into Firenze. We were to spend three nights at the Pensione La Residenza and then leave on August 9th for Pisa. As we needed a map of Florence, I went to obtain one while Lorraine remained with our luggage. When I returned, I found her talking with the husband of our Syrian couple from Rome. He was telling her of a "grand" place where they were staying that was very, very small in price. We went willingly along as he helped us with our suitcases. But soon the buildings we were passing looked quite unkempt. The one he turned into didn't look as if the garbage had been collected in a month of Sundays. It had that certain odor! Up three flights of stairs, we toiled and turned into a black hole. Two fierce dogs and a suspicious landlady greeted us. We quickly decided this was not for us, even at a giveaway price. The landlady sternly demanded our passports. Lorraine was frightened by her threatening manner and would have handed them over, but I refused. I explained we had paid for our first night's lodging at the other hotel and would need them. The landlady realized that this was the last she would see of us once we left, so she and her dogs stamped into her den. (I mean living room.) We continued down the hall to see the wife and baby in their "grand" room. After chatting a while with the couple, we started to examine the papers we had been handed when we entered the building. Strange to say, the landlady had given us a brochure showing a fine old castle with stately halls and quiet rooms at reasonable rates. At first we thought this was false advertisement on her part or a picture of some other place. Then we realized with a start, as we looked at a wall, that the pictured elegant hotel and this dirty, smelly dump really were the exact same place-- but some 20 years apart! We wondered with sadness what had happened during those years. The woman's husband must have died; then paintings faded as dust and grime settled on the walls. And what other tragedies lurked we could not even guess. All we knew for sure was how thankful we were to be out into the sunshine again and pulling our cart toward our Pensione.

Our own hotel did have some minor drawbacks. We were in the attic and the elevator stopped running on the floor below. Also the mosquitoes were thick and hungry. However, the maid sprayed the room to cut down on the insect problem. The place was neat, reasonable and the food was wholesome. At table, we sat with an older couple from Belgium, who were fun to compare notes with on travel. (A little sidelight--most American tourists we noticed drink bottled water at a price. We asked for and got a huge pitcher of ice water for free. I guess we are not typical tourists.)

It is difficult to describe Florence. It definitely is an art city with many beautiful treasures. Yet much has been damaged by moisture or mud wherever the Arno had overflowed. They are still working on restoration, yet the problem of how their bridges dam up the waters has never been solved!

We started our walking tour of Florence with the Cathedral of Santa Maria del Fiore not too far from our hotel. This is the third largest cathedral in the world. It was designed in 1296 and consecrated by Pope Eugene VI in 1436. It is one of the earliest examples of Tuscan Gothic. There are three large bronze doors in the front of the church. A marble relief representing the

Madonna in Glory is above the central one. Inside the church, there is a very different Pieta by Michelangelo. This group is in the shape of a pyramid with Nicodemus following Christ.

The graceful Campanile towers, 82 metres high, was designed and begun by Giotto in 1334. Its delicate decoration with colored marble and its beautiful sets of windows on the upper bands gave the buildings its unity and style. The very lowest panels have carvings depicting the story of the progressive civilization of mankind.

The Baptistry is an octagonal structure with the exterior marble emphasizing geometric forms. The North and South Doors are similar in design and are subdivided into 28 panels illustrating biblical stories. The East Door was called the Gate of Paradise by Michelangelo, who admired its originality. It is the masterpiece of Lorenzo Ghiberti, who worked on it for 27 years, from 1425 to 1452. There are 10 panels in gilt bronze illustrating stories from the Old Testament. Ghiberti's style uses a clear spatial arrangement and an adaptation of perspective which heralds the art of the Renaissance. In our present culture of "the faster the better," it seems incredible to us that someone would take years to create these treasures.

Next we went to one of the most beautiful squares in the world, Piazza Della Signoria. Under the wide arches of the Loggia are numerous statues and many famous masterpieces, including the "Rape of the Sabine Women" by Giambologna in 1583. Inside the Palazzo Vecchio, a massive fortress-like construction, dominating one side of the square, is one of the largest public assembly halls in existence. Massive precious tapestries adorn the four walls. We climbed the back stairs for a closer look at the hangings from a different perspective and also to view the long length of the hall. There are paintings and statues far too numerous to describe scattered throughout this palace. There were so many, many rooms. But the one, which I found most interesting, had 53 maps painted on the cabinet doors and a huge world globe in the center of the room. What an ideal room in which to plan one's travels!

The nearby Church of San Lorenzo is a beautiful example of Florentine Renaissance. Its Chapel of the Princes is overwhelming in its use of precious marbles. Michelangelo designed the New Sacristy which contains the tombs of three members of the Medici family. On one tomb is carved an unusual Madonna with the Child nestled on her breast. The others are matching tombs. In the center niche of one is the Duke idealized as an ancient warrior and on the sarcophagus are symbolic figures of Night and Day. On the other, the Duke is portrayed as a helmeted Roman deep in thought. This sarcophagus is adorned with Dawn and Dusk.

Then a long, long walk to St. Mark's, which houses a museum containing the works of Fra Angelico (1387 - 1455).

We did a great deal of sightseeing this Sunday, in spite of the fact that it was a cloudy, rainy day. Yet we were never wet, for we were either inside gazing at the art or, as it happened during one downpour, we were dining in a fine restaurant. Marvelously, the sun held during all our outside touring.

On Monday, we gained a different view of Florence because we toured the shops. The Ponte Vecchio is a walking bridge literally covered with shops selling gold trinkets, medals, and other expensive jewelry. In fact, in the 14th century it was reserved exclusively for goldsmiths. They set up their shops and built little houses in the back of them that project over the river. No one who comes to Florence can resist this picturesque sight. So the Ponte Vecchio was covered with tourists and we were among them. We also visited other shops and bought some scarves for our mothers. Oh, one more thing, on the street of the leather merchants, Lorraine wanted to buy a finely tooled book bag for my use. But we decided against it because of the price. (Later at home, we regretted our decision as it would have been a great bargain, we realized, when we checked the prices of such articles in California. Ah, well!)

Our shopping spree over, we caught a bus out to the Piazzale Michelangelo. This huge square on the crest of a hill overlooks the entire city of Florence with its red tile roofs. The Cathedral, the Campanile, and the town meeting buildings stood out clearly against the backdrop of distant hills, blue sky and white clouds. It was a gorgeous day and a fabulous view.

Eventually we turned our backs on the view and strolled up the winding road. Finally, we found San Miniato Al Monte. Here we had another adventure. After Mass, we asked one of the priests if we could see the Monastery next door. We could not have asked a better person, for this particular monk was the Abbot! He was a most gracious host and showed us into the huge Abbey. We strolled along the cloister walkway with its slim Ionic columns. The Abbot seemed very interested in the fact that we were from California. He told us that he was going to make a visitation to his monks at Big Sur. They have a retreat house there. So we made up our minds that if we ever had the chance, we would go to Big Sur for a retreat. We had a lengthy conversation with the Abbot and were offered refreshments in the Council room of the Abbey. Thus ended our sojourn in Florence.

Early the next morning, we trundled our luggage cart down the streets, past the Church of St. Maria Novella, and into the Stazione. It was one of those stations where all the trains nosed in, so I called up to one of the engineers, "Which is the train to Pisa?" and he pointed down to track 2. Unfortunately, he thought I had said "Pistoria!" So I checked the board again and Lorraine patiently back-tracked and loaded the suitcases on #8140 waiting on track 8. Once we were aboard, our train backed out at 9:25 a.m. and had us in Pisa at 10:32.

The Leaning Tower of Pisa is a must for every visitor! And for us also. First, a bus ride out to the Piazza del Duomo, and then when we alighted, we beheld a striking sight. To the left of the street were three magnificent marble buildings sitting like enormous white pearls on a green velvet lawn. The first round marble structure was a 12th century Baptistery. Its great pulpit was built by Nicola Pisana. When finally we tore ourselves away from this edifice, we wandered through the 11th century Duomo with its paintings by Andrea del Sarto and Ghirlandaio. Then outside again to gaze in awe at the lean of the Leaning Tower. The Campanile was built in 1173 and developed its slant almost immediately. Recently, it has been slanting about an inch more every 10 years. We watched tourists edging their way around as they inched up higher and higher. It is very dangerous to do this, as there are no guard rails if one should slip. Hugging the inner wall of the Leaning Tower then was a thrill we decided to forego for OBVIOUS REASONS. Therefore, we waved "Goodbye" to this magnificent, airy, open piazza, rightly called the "Meadow of Miracles," and caught our bus back to the train station.

As it was early yet for our 2:48 p.m. train, we had lunch and sat at an outside table people-watching. Many were laughing and enjoying a glass of wine. We thought we would like to enjoy the same. However, the station food service would not sell us a bottle of wine. It was against the law! Strange! Yet everyone was drinking wine. We kept watching and wondering. Suddenly we had an inspiration; we emptied our water canteen, took it to the girl at the counter and silently held it out. She took it and filled it to the brim--with wine! The secret was: bring your own container! We laughed together about this and sipped our wine on a lovely, sunny afternoon in Pisa.

By this time, we were beginning to feel at ease on the trains. I could figure out the track and departures. Ours was the train with the wide yellow stripe under the roof. Also, we quickly learned to identify the non-smoking sections. Each train car always carried its own nameplate. The top name was the city in which the coach originated, then came the important stops, and on the bottom line, the ending city. It was important not only to get on the correct train, but on the correct car also, for they shifted the cars from train to train so quickly and easily that it wasn't noticeable. And you just might find yourself sightseeing in the wrong city! After Rome, we never bothered with reservations. Why pay for a seat when we could read the reservation signs on the doors and pick our own empty compartment right then and there?

Because we wanted to view the Italian Riviera, we chose our seats on the left side of the train going north to Genova. On the right, red roofed towns perched on green hillsides. Great slabs of white Carrera marble were piled high for shipment. On the left were rocky beaches with deep blue water lapping at their edges. We fantasized "what if our California friends, Bernie and Juanita, could sail their little boat from San Francisco Bay to these waters to join the other ships we see bobbing in the warm sunshine?" We could then jump off our train and sail on this inviting Mediterranean Sea. Our dreaming ended abruptly as we changed trains at Genova and then sped along the "Gold Coast" into the French Riviera. Between the train tracks and the sea was a wall-to-wall carpet made of the tops of umbrellas. The sunbathers were packed like sardines in a can. The sight was only broken here and there by a camping section, or a tennis court, or a food stand. So who cares about winning a trip to the French Riviera? Not us!

The apartment houses, however, were bright and colorful with balcony after balcony blossoming with geraniums. And for excitement, inside our train car we discovered we were sharing travel time with a large, lively tour group from Haiti.

We rolled past San Remo and Ventimiglia, pulling into Monte Carlo around 9:30 p.m. We got off the train to look around as passengers from the casinos swarmed onto the train. The train left and we learned that no other trains stopped in Monte Carlo until morning. Thus we had our daring overnight adventure of being locked into the waiting room by a frustrated French-speaking stationmaster. (He did try to find us other lodgings, but failed.) Lorraine was thrilled as the trains rushed by in the night causing a wind to shake the walls of the tiny station. To her this was the ultimate excitement. At 5 a.m. the stationmaster unlocked the door in hopes that we would catch the next train that stopped. Instead, we climbed the hill at the back of the station, up to the Exotic Gardens, and watched the sunrise touch the buildings with gold turning this tiny kingdom into a fairyland. The bay, the ships, the buildings, all had magic at that early hour. We found a bakery and munched on sweet rolls as the sun rose higher. By 8 a.m., we decided to come down off the moutain. We had absorbed the spirit of Monaco and had no desire to "sightsee" through the rooms of the palace. We also learned that no citizen of Monaco could play in the casinos. Very smart move on the part of the king!

We took the next train that quickly went through the busy seaport of Marseilles and on to Avignon. (This seaport had a special interest to me because some fellow classmates and I at Stanford University had been assigned to study Marseilles as a landing site for the Allied invasion during World War II. Our professor was on a government task force in Washington D.C. during the war years. Very hush-hush stuff.)

Mildly rolling hills and well-cultivated farmland marked the French countryside. Avignon is a small town with a tree-lined main street. Its main call to fame seems to be from the tourist trade visiting the summer palace of the popes. We were vastly disappointed in the "so-called palace." Some fading wall paper and a few tiles are all that is left of its former glory. The rest is plain, empty, uninteresting rooms in a large building. Its fate has been ever downward since the time of the popes. It was used as a garrison for French soldiers, then as a prison for awhile. It wasn't worth the price of our francs really. Well now, I shouldn't say that. If we hadn't gone, we might have thought we missed something important.

Back on our journey again, we changed trains in Lyon, finally arriving in Geneve at 9:55 p.m. Would we be able to find our pension at that late hour?

CHAPTER IX
ALPINE MEADOWS AND WATERFALLS

We need not have worried. As we walked out of the train station in Geneve, we saw "Pension Cornavin" in lights in the middle of the block across the street. There we slept the sleep of the exhausted in our comfortable beds. Refreshed the next morning we took a bus out to the United Nations Complex. We didn't quite understand the system of buying tickets at each stop so innocently saved some fares. First we explored a Chinaware Museum on the United Nations grounds. This museum itself is worth a lengthy visit. We had never seen such lovely plates and dinnerware. And so many of them!

Next, we felt like delegates as we were guided through the great halls of the U.N., looked at the murals on the walls, tried out the chairs for size, marveled at their sound-translating system, and wrote postcards in the lobby to keep our folks abreast of world affairs.

Finally, we went over to the World Council of Churches. There we had lunch with the ecumenical delegates! Afterwards we examined their exhibits and prayed in the large chapel there for unity.

This made for a very full morning, and by the time we arrived back at the hotel, it was mid-afternoon. We rested a speck and then started on our walking tour of the central part of Geneve. Would you believe a jet of water coming out of the ground at the rate of 126 miles an hour and rising to a height of 400 feet? Such is the fountain in the Lake of Geneve! We leaned on the bridge by the park to watch this column of water rising high into the air. It surely isn't the prettiest fountain in the world, that is for sure, but it was truly unique!! A little thin and lonely perhaps, but without a doubt spectacular!

Friday, August 12th, was to be another of our long train-ride days. In fact, our train left Geneva at 7:14 a.m. Our hotel lady was a motherly and kind person. She also impressed us with her sense of honesty and concern. When we left this morning before breakfast, she even gave us back some of the money we had paid for breakfast to buy our own meal on the train!

It was still a wee bit early as we traveled in the cool morning air over green hills, around the crescent-shaped Lake Geneve, past the towns of Lausanne and Montreux and into the passes between the lofty mountains. It was only 9:56 a.m. when we arrived in Brig to change trains. At 10:44 we were on our way again, the scenery getting prettier by the minute. It was 11:50 when we walked out of the station at Spiez and gazed down at Lake Thun below. We trundled our cart down the winding road and, of all things, a steamer was loading just as we reached the dock. We parked our luggage and went forward into a lovely dining area where we were given a table on the right side center. As the little boat made its way past charming tiny lakeside docks covered with potted geraniums and other colorful flowers, we feasted on a delicious fish dinner. It was fresh trout, done to perfection. We felt like queens in this peaceful setting, eating our meal leisurely. And the timing was perfect. When we had completely finished eating and were relaxing, the boat docked at Thun!

We crossed over the dock and onto a waiting train. As we settled ourselves comfortably, Lorraine asked what was special to see in Berne, which was our next destination. "Only the bears," I replied. "I could do without the bears," she said and suggested we travel on to Lucerne and our scheduled hotel there for a good night's sleep. As we had gained an hour by catching the noon boat, this was possible. Then, after we settled in at the Hotel Kolping, I studied the train schedule to route us in the morning to Interlaken from Lucerne rather than from Berne.

It was not a main line that took us to Interlaken East the next morning. However, even more surprises awaited us. Our Eurail passes were not good on the Jungfrau Railway as they had been on the Thun boat. Lorraine had gone to get the tickets this time and she nearly died of shock when she heard the price of the tickets. No mistake however!

Jungfrau is a rack railway with the first section opening in 1898, the last section in 1912. The gradients are up to 25%. You change trains three times, and the engines really have to pull. We went up the Jungfrau via the Lauterbrunnen-Kleine Scheidegg-Jungfrajoch route. The mountain stations gave us a chance to view the magnificent scenery as we changed trains. The Junfrau towered over us, tiny midgets, on her lower slopes. The last bit of the journey is through a tunnel cut into the mountain itself. It is 4.4 miles long! Every so often there are side passageways with windows cut into the rock walls. Everyone rushes out of the train trying to see the view but the mist and snow cover the openings.

Finally we disembark onto the highest railway station platform in Europe---11,333 feet!! We are wearing sweaters, scarves, coats, and still we freeze. The temperature is 22; 22 degrees below, that is! The glaciers stretch out for miles. Nearby, tame black birds hop on the glistening white snow. We watched a movie explaining the formation of these mountains. Next, we took an elevator up to the scientific observation laboratory. The view is magnificent in this clear air. This is Switzerland at its breathtaking best. Now we make a personal blunder. We venture into the ice caverns where various statues have been carved out of huge chunks of ice. There were huge ice statues of automobiles, trains, people, etc.... Unfortunately for us there, deep inside the mountain, it is 58 degrees below! Lorraine and I turn blue with the cold. We stagger out numb and faint. Now 22 degrees below is like a spring day. Almost! However, we soon revive and it is time for a breathtaking, beautiful ride back down the Jungfrau via the Grindelwald route. As we rode through the meadows, Lorraine expressed a wish to get a closer look at the wild flowers, thus creating another adventure yet to come.

At Interlaken Ost, we hopped on a regular train and sped back to our Hotel Kolping for a good night's rest after an exhausting but thrilling day. It was so relaxing to be warm and cozy under the comforters on our beds after that chilly cavern.

Sunday, August 14th, and we were only a short walk away from the Cathedral and Mass. Then we explored Luzern. First, the Lowendenkmal, or the Lion Monument, gave us pause for thought. It was carved out of the natural rock in 1821 by Lucas Ahorn to commemorate the Swiss soldiers who fell in the heroic defense of Paris on August 10, 1792. Next, we strolled through the Glacier Garden. Here are deep pits formed by the swirling waters of the melting ice flow. The whirlpool marks are left on the rock walls. Leaving the trees and hillside, we went back to the main part of town browsing in small shops along the way. The Swiss do lovely embroidery work. Climbing a flight of stairs, we found ourselves viewing a Panorama of some important battle. It was a 360 degrees painting on the circular walls of the room with railway cars, military equipment, etc., stretching into the immediate foreground.

We enjoyed the Chapel Bridge and the Mill Bridge much more. The Chapel Bridge spans the River Reuss and was built in 1333 as part of the city's system of fortifications. The interesting sections of this covered bridge are the paintings of incidents in the history of the town on the gables. On the Mill Bridge, the gables are decorated by a series called the "Dance of Death." To lighten our mood, we had fun in a labyrinth of mirrors. Luzern is a clean, beautiful town and we hated to leave it on the 15th as we pulled our luggage cart from the hotel along the walkway skirting the lake, across the modern traffic bridge and into the train station.

Off to Zurich at 10:08 a.m. and a slight wait for our train from Zurich to Innsbruck and Salzburg. Then our train bounced along past lakes and rolling hills. We noted the tiny kingdom of Liechtenstein clinging to the side of a mountain just before we entered Austria.

Salzburg station is a busy railroad center. Signs kept warning us to beware of pickpockets! Not a very hospitable welcome, we thought to ourselves. But Salzburg was full of tourists, as it was just the end of their famous music festival. We found our Pension Adlerhof without difficulty, but everyone within was watching the singers on the T.V.! Supper in their little Cap-restaurant proved tasty to us hungry travelers. Then a quick wash-up found us eager to snuggle under our feather comforters in our pleasant room.

We stayed three nights at our Pension and explored Salzburg all day Tuesday and Wednesday. We visited the churches and found their interiors are quite different from those of Italy. Here are wood carvings rather than marble. The Church offers its treasures for free and the Cathedral plays the Carillon three times a day for the enjoyment of the townspeople. You can be sure we didn't miss a concert. We entered Mozart's house, which is now a museum. It took an afternoon to tour Hellbrunn, an early baroque country palace built in 1613 for Archbishop Marcus Sitticus by Santino Solari. This is a most unusual palace, for the Archbishop had a very unique sense of humor. He would seat his guests around an outdoor banquet table. Then if they became too boisterous from the wine, he would flip a switch and the poor guests would be drenched with water from hidden sprinklers embedded in the table. There were many other similar little devices for "horseplay" scattered about the palace and grounds. There was also a mechanical theater in the pleasure garden, plus many little scenes worked by water flow along the pathways.

We sat in the Residenz Platz and watched the horse carriages trotting by and later on the people hurrying by dressed for the evening performance at the Opera House. (Earlier we had secretly partaken of the hospitality of the Opera House. Its appointments are quite lavish.) As we were people-watching there, we noticed a young man dressed in black evening clothes carrying a briefcase headed for the opera. We overdid the looking and he noticed. As the gentleman came nearer, we told him we were speculating that he must be someone very important: maybe a duke, or a count, or the conductor of the orchestra. He laughed and said, "I am the flute player at the opera tonight." We replied that we had guessed right, he was someone very important!

We had been having some very practical trouble with Lorraine's designer bag. The strap had given way because of the strain of all that we had put inside the bag. Carrying it had become very difficult and stressful. But in Salzburg, we finally found someone in a dress repair shop up the street from our Pension who could fix the luggage strap. What a relief!

Packed and out on the morning of the 18th to catch the 10:12 a.m. train for Melk and Vienna. At the railway station, Lorraine befriended an elderly couple as they struggled with their luggage. The woman spoke only a little English. Gradually their story unfolded. The husband had lost his leg when only 18 years old during the German-Russian War. She had been exiled to Siberia for 6 years. They were both Jewish and were among the first to emigrate to Israel. Unfortunately, they were on the boat that was quarantined by the British in the port for two long months. They had had many troubles, but this couple's love for each other and their sense of bravery and humor about catastrophes sparked our admiration.

We got off together at Melk and decided to stay in the Bahnhof Hotel here for the next two nights, as it would be cheaper to commute back and forth to Wein than to try for a hotel in the capital. Sure enough the wife, by speaking German, obtained a very nice room at a very reasonable rate for us. True, the lock on the bath door wouldn't work and our bedroom walls vibrated with the sound of the conductor across the street shouting the trains all night. But on the plus side, there were soft, warm down comforters on our beds and the windows were double glass to keep out the cold.

We trudged through the ancient streets of Melk with its red-roofed burgers' houses dating from the Renaissance period. Past old towers and the remains of the town wall, we climbed up the hill to the largest and most impressive Baroque Abbey we had ever seen. The Benedictine Abbey is immense and it dominates the town and the countryside from its position crowning the hill overlooking the Danube River. It is the most perfect baroque structure in Europe. There is a marble hall with allegorical paintings on the ceilings. The colors, especially the blues in "Reason Guiding Humanity," are just as vivid as when they were painted in 1732 by Paul Troger. One can imagine the monks pondering over the thousands of books in the Bibliothek. The Abbey Church (Steftskirche) sits squarely in the center, with arms of the Abbey stretching out on either side. Inside is a magnificent pipe organ that is still used for concerts today. Above the high altar, Peter and Paul are taking leave of one another as we gazed upward at this painting from the nave of the church. Outside once more, we lean on the railing of the terrace to look down at the boats on the blue Danube below. Later, as we returned down the hill, we crossed a little bridge and explored an island in the river which is used as a site for picnics and for camping.

Friday, August 19th, was a very strenuous sightseeing day in Vienna. It was a wise move on our part, however, that we finally decided to take an official tour of the city. We saw more of the buildings of Vienna in three hours than we could have in three days on our own. We ate our lunch while riding on the bus and were surprised that it was 1:30 p.m. when the tour ended.

Schonbrunn, the summer palace, was started in 1695 by Emperor Leopold I. But it was Empress Maria Theresa who, besides running the country and rearing 16 children (11 girls and 5 boys), still had time to redecorate the interior! It had been baroque and she wanted rococo. Finally we can tell the difference between the two styles. Baroque is symmetrical and rococo is asymmetrical. The palace rooms are very ornate with white walls and goldleaf trim. One was done in Chinese black lacquer, Chinese prints, and Oriental vase; another had Indian prints against walnut wood paneling. Outside, across a long green expanse of lawn, is an enormous classical stone arch called the "Gloriette" to commemorate some victory. Interestingly enough, 2,200 people still live in the Schonbrunn Palace even today. Actually, only 45 rooms are on view for tourists. All the outside walls are painted yellow with white trim. Maria Theresa thought this color scheme would make the huge palace look cheery on dreary, rainy, winter days.

Belvedere Palace belonged to Prince Eugene and now is used as an art gallery. We also walked through the Imperial Rooms at the Hofburg. Frans Josef's wife was Elisabeth and she decreed "No more portraits of her" once she reached the age of 30! She was assassinated when she was 63 in Geneve by an insane man. She was an early believer in physical fitness, and she had her own personal gym for daily workouts.

As Vienna (Wien) grew over the years to now over a million inhabitants, many different styles of architecture were used in their fine public buildings like the Parliament, the Opera House, the museums etc. But also Wien established a unique system that is very helpful to visitors in locating these sites. All the city's most important buildings, monuments, and other sights are marked by small shields with flags in the city's colors. Thus it is easy to identify at a glance the interesting buildings and to obtain a few historical details.

We just had to visit the world-famous Lipizzaner stallions and the Spanish Riding School. The great hall with its priceless chandeliers, where the horses perform their classical precision steps, was a grand sight. But who would expect the horses to have marble stalls with shiny brass fixtures! We patted the stallions while a ham actor or two among them showed off for us visiting humans. Yes, we were impressed!

Then off to the churches! We walked to the Franciscan with a full-sized painting of Leonardo da Vinci's "Last Supper" covering one wall. This beautiful copy was painted by Fracono Raffaeli between 1806 and 1814. Next was the Augustian Church with an exquisite cenotaph for Archduchess Maria Christine done by Antonio Canova between 1798 and 1805. This was the most moving tribute to a woman, who loved the poor, that we have ever seen. The hungry and the disabled were making their way to Maria Christine. It was a remarkable tribute and a touching monument.

Finally we reached St. Stephen's. This cathedral had been partly destroyed in the war by bombs. It has been restored by funds raised from the various sections of the country. Poor Austria has been under occupation for about 15 years: first, under Hitler, and then under the Allies. The people here are hardworking and friendly but not as prosperous as the Swiss, nor as secure!

Retracing our steps from St. Stephen's, we rested on a park bench in front of the Raushaus (town hall) for an hour, listening to a band concert. Then back to Melk on the 7:20 p.m. train.

On Saturday morning, we bid goodbye to the elderly couple and wished them a safe trip. We had decided to move on and took our suitcases with us to Vienna. We rode through the Vienna Woods and the charming countryside for the last time. Once back in Wien, we took streetcar #18 to the Sud Bahnhof. What a clumsy system of transferring from one train station to another! After checking our luggage, we figured out the bus system to the museums on either side of Queen Maria Theresa's platz. These buildings, with their broad marble staircases, looked more like palaces to us than had the actual royal palaces. The Natural History Museum had a fantastic display of rocks, insects, birds, and other animals. One could spend a week just looking at the various rock collections alone. We walked across the platz, past the Queen's statue and into the Fine Arts Museum. Here we were most impressed by the beauty of the glassware on display. Earlier, passing a store, we had watched an artist etching glass. When the museums closed, back we went to the Sudbahnhoff. We had a delicious vegetable salad in the outdoor cafe, wrote postcards to our parents, and embarked on the waiting train by 4 p.m. We felt that we had thoroughly "toured" Vienna and were justifiably tired.

Actually, we were a day ahead of our schedule. We had a dream in mind, however, and we discussed its possibilities as we rode through the grape-growing country and into the mountains. As the train began to climb higher, we asked the conductor's advice. He recommended Murzzuschlag, about

74 miles from Vienna to view the wild flowers. We were so eager about our adventure that we almost hopped off the train at a remote mountain siding, but the conductor motioned us back onto the train just in time. About 6 p.m., he reassured us that this was actually the right spot to leave the train. Pulling our suitcases through the main street in the little town, we located a small family hotel. After asking for a room with a view, we landed snugly in the attic with the breathtaking vista of the mountains from our windows. Our supper at the hotel consisted of the best food we had eaten so far in Austria.

Sunday morning, the 21st, we awoke fresh for our free adventure day. First, we went to the beautiful parish church for Mass. The building was in simple baroque style using black ebony marble and gold angels. The main altar was green and rose marble with a glistening gold tabernacle with gold angels keeping guard.

Leaving the church, we walked across a bridge and into the silent woods along the Murz River. It was a physical fitness trail, bounded by lush ferns and overhanging trees. And we were the sole walkers. The wild flowers were unbelievable: wild cyclamen, white, yellow, purple, blue, even rose color; other flowers of all kinds and shapes, and ferns of every description. A bend in the trail and a sudden view of the lofty mountains rose steeply around us. Clear, sparkling water in the river, cold as ice, hurried past us. A piece of God's Paradise was shared there with us. Three hours passed as one moment, but they became an eternal treasure to have and to hold in the heart. Little had we suspected that God would grant Lorraine's wish for a closer look at the wild flowers in such a lovely, charming setting.

A very different sort of experience had awaited us at lunch. The menu was beyond our comprehension. Lo and behold, another "Joseph" gallantly came to our rescue. This gentleman had been a professional English soldier who had served here during the occupation. He had fallen in love with an Austrian girl, married her, and settled down in Murzzuschlag upon retiring. Last year she died so he was lonely now. Because of the cost of living, he had a job driving workers to the factory some miles away. He insisted that he would drive us to the train station tomorrow. Well, if it is raining at noon time, that would be a blessing. So far the rain has never been a hindrance to us. It only rains when we are indoors visiting a museum, or eating, or sleeping at night. However, the weather is turning colder. We wore our sweaters and coats on our hike today--a far cry from the hot desert lands of Israel.

In the late afternoon, the rain settled in. From our attic windows, we watch the dark clouds catch hold of the tall green firs on the mountainsides. The church bells ring out the quarter hours. Inside warm and dry, we rest and write to our dear ones.

This was just the night we decided to make our own soup and cheese sandwiches in our cozy room. Flicking on the T.V., we discovered educational television in Austria. One program showed clear close-ups of the treasures and carved wood in the Salzburg Cathedral. It was a thrill to see the sights, that we had strained upwards to see, brought down to our eye level. We enjoyed other views of the country, a tour through a museum, and an arts and crafts show before falling asleep. If only we could spend a week in this lovely place.

LUCILLE HINTZE

CHAPTER X
RAIN, DARK GLASSES AT MIDNIGHT AND VENICE

Well, our soldier of fortune had to work, so around noon we trundled our suitcases to the train station to board the train for Venice. The train rolled out of the mountains and into the lake country around Klagenfurt and Villach. The heavy mist outside turned into a torrential downpour and the hour grew later and later. Eight p.m. and our normal arrival time in Venice came and went. So did 9, 10, 11 and midnight! Finally our train arrived in the darkened station at 1 a.m. in the morning. The few passengers quickly scattered while we were getting our luggage together. A short, wiry man wearing dark glasses came up and told us he would take us to our hotel in his boat. He insisted "just follow me" as he turned left toward the darker part of the platform. The thought hit me. Arthur said "GO RIGHT!" Lorraine agreed with me and we turned to the right carrying our luggage. The man kept pace with us, arguing and insisting almost up to the dim lights of the dock. We kept replying, "No! No!" Just at that moment the vaporetto slid up and we quickly jumped in with our luggage. Were we ever grateful for "Uncle Arthur" telling us about the public motorboat transportation system! That man probably would have charged us a much more expensive price for the ride, we thought to ourselves. Leaving the fuming "dark glasses" far behind on the darkened platform, we traversed the silent canals of Venice and landed on the very doorstep of our hotel. We rang the night bell and were escorted to our rooms.

The next morning we were telling the concierge of our midnight arrival and the man with the dark glasses who had wanted us to ride in his boat. The concierge got a very strange look on his face and called over an official-looking gentleman. They rapidly conversed in Italian and then this official asked us many questions about the man with the dark glasses. Shaking his head, he muttered that we were very, very fortunate women. Then he told us in plain English why we were so fortunate. We were in shock! Arthur had not merely saved us a few dollars, he had saved our lives! Did we send up fervent prayers of gratitude to heaven! We were two very sober people at breakfast that morning.

The Savio and Jolana Hotel, where we spent three nights, was a most comfortable establishment. Not only that, it was only a short walk away from all the action: St. Mark's Square, the Bridge of Sighs, churches, shops, palaces, and everything else. Venice is a charming island sharing its treasures with us. When I say we toured Venice, I really mean we did not miss a sight. First and foremost, of course, was the enormous Basilica of St. Mark. Behind the high altar was a gold screen called the Pala d'oro. It is a work of goldsmith craftsmanship started in 1071 and finally finished in the 14th century. There are figures of the holy men and women of God enriched with gems, pieces of enamel and studded with gold. Our heads reeled from seeing so much glitter and gold.

Next, we climbed up into the vast gallery to get a closer look at the mosaics that took 700 years to complete. The vaulting illustrates the story of Creation, Cain and Abel, Abraham, even to "Salome's Dance" in the Baptistry. The Last Judgment, I think by Titian, was impressive. If one doesn't feel dizzy looking down, the bizarre patterns in the floor come into focus. Then a sad reflection on human nature came in the midst of all this beauty, some young people were scribbling on the walls. I went over and spoke to them about defacing the mosaics but they could care less about destroying what took years to construct.

Also up in the gallery, we edged past the large bronze horses and looked over the railing at the tiny people far below in the Piazza. The pigeons circled and landed to be fed. High above on the roof of the Clock Tower, two men of bronze strike at the huge bell between them to mark the passing hours.

Public buildings, Doge's Palace, the Bridge of Sighs and old prison cells, tiny bridges spanning waterways, we saw everything. We even took the motorboat ride along the Grand Canal and out as far as the Lido. Once we saw a wedding party in their decorated gondolas.

We walked through different sections of the city visiting churches, some of which have been converted into museums. We were sorry to see so much evidence of decay in many buildings. Still much, much beauty in Venice remains. And, for the fortunate shopper, beautiful embroidery and lace await. Glassware in every color, shape, and form just ask to be admired. Magnificent glass sculptures virtually turn stores into modern glass art galleries.

LUCILLE HINTZE

CHAPTER XI
BACK TO HILL COUNTRY

All too soon it was time to catch our vaporetto back to the station where train #842, the Santa Lucia, waited at the early hours of 7:26 a.m. to whisk us to Milan. There, discovering that there was no train to Zurich for a couple of hours, we decided to hop on the first train going north. This was the Metropolitano, headed for Basel and Karlsruhe, Germany. But no real problem here if we remembered to get off at Arth-Goldau.

Glorious scenery delighted us along the way. Our first traveling companion was an Italian cruise ship captain who looked and acted the part.

In the course of our conversation, he told us of the trouble on container ships. So many people stole from the containers that the companies shipped all left shoes in one container and then the right in another. But still, he said that people stole the shoes. At this point Lorraine and I glanced down at our sandals and almost burst out laughing. She had two left sandals on her feet and I had on two right! After our sophisticated captain got off in Como, we quickly exchanged our sandals. Then we made our way to the dining car by hopping off the train at a stop, running back ten cars and hopping back on the train at the dining car. But this meal was worth it! Excellent food, picture windows and glorious scenery from Chiasso and Lugano north. Waterfalls tumble down mountainsides as we roll along the pass. This was our first meal aboard a train. And it proved to be one of our memorable occasions where everything turned out just right. When finally we hurried back to our own car, lurching and weaving with the jolting motion of the speeding train, we laughed in sheer joy. Lorraine even helped an elderly lady with her suitcase, but the lady wasn't quite sure that Lorraine wasn't a train robber taking her bag! So we had something more to laugh about.

Changing trains at Arth-Goldau, we soon were passing contented cows grazing on rolling green hills. We got so bewitched by the scenery that we hopped off the train at Hersau instead of St. Gallen. Didn't discover the mistake until I went across the street to a little shop to buy another stocknagel and it said Hersau on it! (I had purchased a walking cane for my mother in Austria. Then we discovered that the walkers picked up these little souvenirs at the various different towns to show where they had been. Nailed on, these would make the walking cane a very interesting conversation piece. Hopefully, this would overcome my mother's prejudice about using a cane. So I reasoned anyway.) I walked back to Lorraine and the luggage. Would you believe it? This was our first error and there was only a 10 minute delay! We jumped right back on the next passing train, to the conductor's amazement, who then made a point of coming to our compartment to tell us when we arrived in St. Gallen, as if we would possibly make the same mistake twice! Or could we?

Our hotel was supposed to be an easy two blocks from the station, but we wandered around for over two hours. Finally I exclaimed "I'm tired!" Lorraine quickly answered, "Why didn't you say so? Here's our hotel now!" She claims she was just showing me the sights of St. Gallen. But I think luck was with her at that point. Anyway, we had explored practically every other street in the little town.

Our real reason for coming to St. Gallen was not the beauty of this lovely town, but the fact that it is near to Pestalozzi Children's Village at Trogen. In August of 1944, Walter Corti suggested to the Swiss people the idea of building a village home for the needy children of many countries orphaned in the Second World War. The village was named after Johann Heinrich Pestalozzi, the great humanitarian (1746-1827) who insisted that the family home was the starting point of all real education, that the harmonizing of mind, body and soul was the birthright of every child, as well as the tolerance and acceptance of different individuals. The little community of Trogen donated the hilltop land and the Children's Village began to take shape.

At first there were Austrian, French, Polish, Hungarian, Italian, Finnish and Greek children. British children arrived in 1950. Fourteen to eighteen children live in the style of a family under the supervision and care of their house parents, who are always a married couple of the same nationality. Mornings are reserved for national teaching in the children's houses. In the afternoon, they attend international courses, where mixed groups of all nations work together. The two principal aims are to help children in need and distress and to be a place of meeting and cooperation, a center of mutual understanding beyond all national, religious, and linguistic barriers.

After the European war, the orphans grew up and established families of their own. The village then expanded to include countries outside of Europe. Tibetan refugee children arrived in 1960; Korean and Tunisian in 1965; Vietnamese in 1972; and Ethiopian in 1974. So the work goes on.

Friday morning found us on the small electric train, only two cars long, climbing the hillsides to Trogen. The view was glorious; wide vistas of green mountains, tiny villages with houses colorful with bright red geraniums in window boxes. Even the gables were decorated.

On the electric train we started chatting with a Canadian lady who is married to a Swiss man. She invited us to her home and explained much more about the Children's Village. Then she took us outside and pointed out a tiny foot path winding up the hillside through the grass towards the buildings at the top. This would be a shortcut to the village, she told us. We took the path, climbed the hill, and then visited the village. It is a remarkable place for children, very well run, while still very loving and homelike. Afterwards we walked down the paved road on the other side to Trogen below. At the turn of the road, we sat down on a bench, and just absorbed the beautiful view. These children surely grow up in a choice site.

In the town, we visited the lovely Fraukirche with all its pictures and statues of the Blessed Mother. Even the confessionals had small statues or busts on top of them to add to the beauty of the church. The ceiling pictures of the Assumption and of the Coronation of Mary were very well done in blue, green, and gold leaf. Then it was back to St. Gallen via our electric train.

While I packed for Saturday's early departure, Lorraine ventured forth to buy a box of candy for the Blantons and she surprised me with a tiny box containing two pieces of the most delicious candy I have ever eaten in my whole life. Such a luscious memory! Swiss candy is dated. No one eats day old chocolates. (Even yet, our candy seems tasteless when I compare it to their chocolates. We have too many preservatives which makes for a flavor change in our foods.)

August 27th was a long train-riding day. However, we were well fortified by a filling Swiss breakfast, the best day-starter in all Europe. We left St. Gallen at 8:48 a.m. and arrived at 9:58 in Zurich. As we pulled into the station, we debated whether to get off on the right or left side of the coach. We decided on the left. A most fortunate choice! For the signboard on the train next to us said "Basle!" Lorraine lifted our suitcases on board, and immediately the train began to back out. It was 10:05! If we had unloaded on the right side, we would not have been able to walk clear around our St. Gallen train in time to catch the one for Basle.

A short hour's ride found us ready for sightseeing in Basle. Unfortunately, the overcast turned into a slight drizzle as we walked along the banks of the Rhine. Its waters looked gray and cold. Arriving at the Munsterplatz, we found the cathedral there to be a perfectly proportioned building of dark red sandstone. It was first built in the 11th century and contains the tombs of Queen Anne and Erasmus. Nearby was the Kunst Museum, in which we lingered much longer than we would have had the weather been better. The Museum featured a large, rather weird painting of a mermaid with long red hair sitting on a rock with a dead merman floating beneath in the water. A very strange composition! After all the beautiful art we have seen, this painting did not seem worthy to us to hang in a museum.

We left Basle from the Bahnhof at 4:53 on the Metropolitano bound for Karlsruhe. It was dark by the time we pulled into Karlsruhe at 6:43 p.m. Were we happy to see the Blantons waiting for us! (These were friends from the parish in which Lorraine had worked. Guy had been in the Navy and when he retired from the service, he went into the Red Cross work.)

LUCILLE HINTZE

CHAPTER XII
ADVENTURES IN GERMANY

Guy and Mickie had a lovely upstairs apartment at the military post in Stuttgart called Patch Barracks. Sunday, August 28th, we went to Mass, talked, visited Guy's Red Cross office, went through the Post Exchange, and talked some more.

Monday morning, bright and early, 8 a.m. to be exact, Mickie, Guy, Lorraine and I piled into a car and started south down Highway 8 and 7. As we rode along the rolling countryside, we could see the spires of the great cathedral at Ulm looming up for miles. We passed through Kempten and Fussen and enjoyed our picnic lunch on the grounds of Hohenschwangau. We had arrived in Mad King Ludwig's land. Guy just ran up the pathway to the medieval-style gray granite castle but we three women, not into physical fitness at the moment, elected to ride up the steep roadway in a horse-drawn carriage. Neuschwanstein Castle, with its towers and pinnacles, soars upward amid the surrounding lofty mist-enveloped peaks of Bavaria. Such a setting creates a castle of daydreams. Everywhere throughout the entire structure from walls to wash basins, the swan motif is used. From this charming castle, we traveled east to the Wieskirche. The forest suddenly opens and there is a church sitting on a hilltop in the middle of a pasture. The outside of the building seemed ordinary enough, but stepping inside we were completely overawed by the sheer beauty of the interior. Color and line are harmoniously combined. The first dominating color is a wonderfully tinted red appearing in the stucco columns to the left and to the right of the altar. This symbol of our being redeemed by Christ's sacred blood is then transformed into the brilliancy of a festive Easter Allelujah. The second dominating color is a special blue, symbolizing God's blessing and grace coming down to us on earth. Zimmermann, the architect, employed the moving and periodically circling light of the sun as an element of the building. This is the reason that this church is so remarkable among churches. Also, there is but one door to Wies Church. Stepping inside and raising one's eyes, overwhelming beauty uplifts the spirit. The church, built to house the "statue of Christ bound to the pillar that wept," extolls the blessings gained thus for us. Upon leaving the church, one looks upwards to the painting of the "door of eternity" which is still closed but some day will open into the splendors of "eternal life."

But now one must go out the lower door into the world. But such a world! The vista of the Tannheim Range, the Trauch Mountains with dark forest, the green meadows, the azure blue of the sky, and the floating white clouds holds one enchanted. Such beauty inside and out!

We drove through Oberammergau where the villagers reenact the Passion Play every ten years. In late afternoon, we reached the Abbey Church of Ettal. This monastery was founded by King Ludwig the Bavarian in gratitude for help received. The ancient legend relates that a gray robed monk had promised that aid would come and gave the king a small marble statue of Our Lady. The first church was a twelve-sided building consecrated in 1370. Monks, plus knights with their ladies, were attached to the Abbey. Ettal became a place of pilgrimage visited by thousands. However, a change in fortune came during the next three hundred years. The

Monastery endured poverty, invasions, murders, plundering, and burning. The monks often had to take refuge, with their statue, in the mountains. The church was partly destroyed. Finally in 1762, the church was completely rebuilt and consecrated anew. The present interior gives the impression of a circular building because of simple, clustered columns in the angles of the polygon. Your gaze is directed upwards. No horizontal plane breaks this upward sweep except the wide cornice below the windows, which forms an accentuated, intentional break. The symbolic composition of the paintings are spiritually and artistically masterpieces. Ettal is a church with quite a history.

That night we checked into the General George S. Patton Hotel at Garmisch. The next morning, a Tuesday, we traveled through the glorious Alpine country of Berchtesgaden. Around noon, we took a boat ride on the Konigsee, a magnificent jewel of crystal clear green water. The gray stone mountains, with patches of verdant pasture land clinging at precipitous angles, rise up at 90 degree angles out of the water. Our boat stopped in the middle of this quiet lake and a bugler played. The sound streamed across the waters and echoed back from the mountains. This was a treat for the ears!

This German fjord is five miles long and at its end is a tiny dock, a church and a restaurant where they featured fresh pork. The pork was indeed very, very fresh! As we walked around the buildings, we heard excited voices. Three men were herding one huge fat pig into a small slaughterhouse attached to the kitchen of the restaurant. Without a doubt that pig suspected his fate!

On our way back from the lake, we could see high above us the gray stone Eagle's Nest, Hitler's mountain stronghold. What a day! Our overnight accommodations here were at the General Walker Hotel. The Blantons gave us the thrill of our lives by installing us in the General's suite having a sitting room no less, as well as a bedroom! Through the windows, we could view the rugged mountain peaks with the black storm clouds swirling over their rocky crests. Those cold winds blowing off the icy peaks had no effect on us. We snuggled down under pure wool blankets in our two luxurious double beds in our fabulous rooms.

Next morning we hurried past Rosenheim and on to Munchen. We did arrive in time to see the Glockenspiel figures perform at 11 a.m. in the clock tower. We wandered about in the plaza. Tasty, circular, bratwurst in the open air cafe there added to our enjoyment and gave us strength to continue our journey. The Gothic Frauenkirche with its two onion-shaped domes was only a short walk away and also St. Peter's, with gleaming white and gilt rococo inside. It doesn't look its age. Imagine, it was actually begun in 1050 and is the oldest parish church in Munich. Now that is aging with grace!

It was modern freeway driving all the way to Augsburg, where we went to the most interesting and oldest Senior Citizen Village in the world. In 1519, Fuggerei established a complex in the city for elderly poor. Each apartment has four rooms. They were simple but very adequate. Fuggerei endowed the place with all his wealth and, even today, the people pay only about 41 cents a year rent. This was a truly remarkable act of social concern so many years ago for needy families. It would be great if someone would do the same today in our own country.

Back at the Blanton's home, we unloaded the car and then went to the Officers' Club for dinner. This is very noteworthy because here we had our first real red meat since leaving USA. In Israel and Europe, the average person does not consume meat as we do in our country.

Thursday, Mickie took us to Heidelberg. This town is famous for three things: the old Heidelberg Castle now in ruins; Schwetzingen, governmental seat and the most beautiful castle gardens in Germany; and tender, mouthwatering asparagus. We sampled all three! There is no way one can describe those acres and acres of beautiful gardens, groves of trees, and various statuary placed at strategic points. But two interesting and very unusual spots can be mentioned: first of these was a circular wire affair on top of which there are many metal birds of various types that spout water into a pool in the center of this enclosed walkway; and second, at the end of an arbor there was a curious optical illusion that gives one the idea of an endless vista. I don't know how they did this.

In old Heidelberg, the most interesting section was the German Pharmacy Museum. One old green wooden pharmacist's cupboard has paintings of convents built in the 17th and 18th centuries on its upper door panels. There is also a genealogical tree which grows out from the paintings of the monastic grounds in Munich and spreads out over the other paintings and symbolizes the history of the monastic foundation in the provinces of South Germany. The history of medicine is depicted in this museum showing druggist equipment, medicines of plant, animal and mineral origin, plus ancient books. There were also some beautiful glass containers, profusely decorated, cut and painted mainly with alchemic symbols.

Another side tour we took, this time with both Guy and Mickie, was to St. Peter's Church at Bad Wimpfen next to the Neckar River. By the 7th century, this site already had a church. However, the construction of the present Gothic Church began in 1269. The beautiful stained glass windows like those in southern Germany depict scenes from both the Old and New Testaments. To the left of the middle window is the oldest statue of St. Francis north of the Alps. Francis died in 1226 and this figure was sculptured in 1274. That is not even 50 years after his death. Francis must have been well known and truly loved.

While we were there, a baby was baptized in the Sacramental Chapel. The young parents were so proud of their child and the Benedictine Monk so reverent and concerned. We admired the baby and congratulated the parents. After the parents and the baby left, this monk showed us around the cloister and gardens. He had been in a concentration camp along with other priests. Out of 48 priests in the camp, 36 died there. Only 12 were still alive when the Russians came. After World War II, even this tiny remainder of the Benedictines were expelled from East Germany. Settling in Bad Wimpfen, they undertook the task of restoring the old church and cloister to their original state of exquisite beauty. During the Middle Ages, the Benedictine Fathers were missionaries, schoolmasters, agriculturists, historians, and theologians. Today's duties are much the same, except their ministerial offices are performed in high schools, social welfare departments, and jails. We were much impressed by the genuine piety of this Benedictine. That particular priest truly exemplified the ancient Benedictine motto: "That God may be glorified in all things."

Well, so much was happening while with the Blantons that we stayed an extra day. We reluctantly left Stuttgart on the fast Trans-European Train "Merkur" at 7:06 a.m. on September 3rd, a Saturday. The sky was dark, overcast, and misty. But the threatening rain and fog burned off just about the time we boarded the Rhine steamer at Mainz. We were going to "do" the most interesting section of the Rhine River by the slower means of boat travel. We leisurely moved down the Rhine at about 10 knots an hour, having plenty of time to gaze at the castles perched on the cliffs, examine the countryside of hills and vineyards, and to enjoy the view of the picturesque towns clinging to the shores. This was truly the "Rhine Cruise," no different than a luxury liner, except in price. Wandering musicians entertained us. Guides announced spots of interest. We enjoyed our picnic lunch while admiring the forts and churches along the beautiful Rhine. Nothing was wanting, except the Rhine Wine which was, of course, too astronomical for our pocketbook.

At Koblenz, which is situated at the meeting point of the Rhine, Moselle, and Lohn Rivers, we had two hours free, just enough time to visit the Castor Cathedral (836 A.D.) and the Florinskirche (1200), before embarking on our train for Trier. The Moselle River Valley is a quiet, peaceful rolling hill area as compared to the strong, majestic Rhine. After a 1 1/2 hour ride, we found our Hotel Kurfurtz Baldwin at 7:13 p.m. It had been a long, long day and our beds felt mighty good.

Trier is "the" oldest city in Germany. The Romans occupied the site in the 2nd century. Of their town, a spectacular arch called the Porta Nera, still remains. In the 4th century, a Romanesque Cathedral, now the oldest in Germany, was built. The year 1235 saw the erection of the Liebfraen, first Gothic church of Germany. But, although we saw all these impressive sights, none of them were our reasons for traveling to Trier. Early Sunday morning, we rode the bus up this street and down that until finally we arrived at a modest church on the outskirts of the town. Here our pilgrimage ended at the tomb of St. Matthew. Now we have prayed at the shrines of both our Apostle Friends, Mark and Matthew.

CHAPTER XIII
ONWARD TO PARIS

Back at the hotel, we hurriedly packed and headed for the railway station and the noon train to Paris. Well actually, as we had given up Luxembourg, we had to take a train first to Saabrucken, next to Metz, and then on to Paris. It seemed as though we rumbled for hours through that great city, arriving around 7 p.m. Actually, there was an hour time change that we had not realized. Fortunately, as we stepped off the train, there was Nicole still waiting patiently for us! Will wonders never cease? She squeezed us and our luggage into her little car and we were off for a night tour of gay Paree.

Nicole was a wonderful guide. Because of her, we really saw all of Paris. It is an enormous, and crowded city, with teeming thousands of people and cars. After her morning classes, Nicole took us sightseeing. We drove along the broad Avenue des Champs-Elysees, both by night and day, marveling at its buildings and shops. Nicole circled the Arc de Triomphe three times so that we could get a closer look at the bas reliefs. We saw the Invalides (soldiers' hospital), the Tomb of Napoleon, and the Army Museum. At the south end of the Avenue, the tall obelisque marked the Place de la Concorde. Next was the Louvre, the greatest museum of the fine arts in the world, housed in a huge former palace. One could spend a month within its walls. We, however, could spend only a full morning there. We thrilled to see the originals of our Holy Family favorites: the Angelus and the Gleaners by Millet. That afternoon, Nicole and her aunt took us out to Versailles. Here Louis XIV lived with 1,500 nobles in his court. The great hall has been used even in modern times for important treaties. But the king needed to retire from the pressures of state affairs, so he had two more palaces built. The larger, pink marble one, is called the Grand Trianon; the smaller, the Petit Trianon. A little pastoral village, called by Marie Antoinette "le petit hameave," occupied a rustic section of the grounds. Here Marie and her maids pretended they were simple country lasses. There are woods and lakes. The extensive gardens at Versailles stretch for miles. We were thoroughly exhausted from just walking through them!

Next, a very special treat for us was arranged by Nicole and her aunt. We waited for a little restaurant called "Toone" to open. There was a delay because the help inside were celebrating! But once inside, delicious crepes were served piping hot, baked on special irons. The French have the gold medal for crepes, as the Swiss do for their chocolate candy! Mouth watering!

Our own "Trianon Palace Hotel" was very comfortable and within easy walking distance of the Louvre, Notre Dame which we visited twice, and other points of interest. Notre Dame is one of the most beautiful Gothic churches we have visited. Outside you are awed by the flying buttresses. Going closer, you marveled at the magnificently carved portals. The central one is of the "Last Judgment." The one on the right is "St. Ann's Portal" and the one on the left is "The Blessed Virgin Mary's." Once inside, two vivid rose windows take your breath away. The predominantly blue-toned window has been intact since the 13th century, although the rose-toned one has had to have some restoration. Their beauty has remained undiminished over the centuries. A statue of the Virgin of

Notre Dame de Paris dates from the 14th century, along with a series of wood inlaid with gold bas-reliefs, depicting scenes from the life of Christ.

Then we left the crowd to be invited through the barriers into the choir section enclosing the High Altar. Here we attended a special Latin Gregorian High Mass sung by a monsignor and a male choir. It was a most beautiful Mass in a most beautiful church. All this peace and beauty for us, eleven in all, while outside in the rest of the church, thousands of tourists came and went. This was a very special gift from God to us in France.

Our morning walks along the Seine River gave us much of the color of gay Paree. The art galleries, the tiny stalls, the flower stands, all added to the glamor. We crossed the Pont Neuf, the oldest bridge in the city, laughing at its weird carved heads of very hairy and bearded men. We stopped to watch, fascinated, the setting of cobblestones to form a pavement. The laborer was a master artist, swiftly picking up a stone, tossing it up with a sharp clip or two, and behold, fitting it exactly into its niche with a bit of sand. We hurried through the dreary Conciergerie-- a palace turned prison. We felt rejuvenated in the airy Sainte Chapelle with its stained glass window walls depicting Biblical scenes. We strolled through the Latin Quarter, visiting the Pantheon now used for art and the theater, and the Maison de Victor Hugo with his numerous sketchings used to illustrate his novels. We mingled with the students hurrying to classes down the ancient corridors of the Sorbonne. We were "at one with" the heart of the great French Universite.

Lorraine said, "I have a dilemma." "So...," I answered.

"My dad told me we ought to go to the Folies Bergeres in Paree."

"It is your decision. Maybe you ought to check with the concierge about prices and tickets to help you make up your mind." I wondered what she would decide as Lorraine disappeared downstairs. She soon returned bearing two large, oversized postcards in her hands. "Solved! Here is a postcard on the Folies that I will send to my folks and here is one on Notre Dame for you to send to your mother." (I was very relieved because I didn't want to have to tell her we didn't have enough money for even half a ticket.)

On Wednesday afternoon, Nicole's little car trudged up the steep and winding road around the hill of Montmaire. When luckily a tiny parking space was found, we got out and walked up to the Sacre Coeur Church perched on the hilltop. This is the site where St. Ignatius and his first companions, who were students studying at the Sorbonne, agreed to band together to form the Society of Jesus. Above the main altar is a magnificent and compelling mosaic of Christ with outstretched arms. "Bring all peoples to me," he seems to say. We knelt in prayer at the exposition of the Blessed Sacrament that day. Prayed for our parents and, in particular, for all travelers.

Outside, a panoramic view of this enormous city overwhelmed us. It stretched out as far as the eye could see in all directions. Although arrows pointed out the various public buildings, the Eiffel Tower was the only one we recognized immediately.

On the drive back, Nicole gave us a closer view of these beautiful churches and magnificent public buildings. That evening we dined with Nicole and her aunt in their modest apartment. However, it was located in a high-rise complex that houses 3,000 people! There are batteries of elevators. Each has a special route. You have to know exactly which one and then where to take the second one, or you are hopelessly lost in the vast reaches of the enormous building. It is mind-boggling. Yet, once inside their apartment, the atmosphere is homey. Nicole's aunt was a most gracious hostess and served a delicious supper. Once again we were grateful for becoming friends with this vivacious French professor during our stay in Jerusalem. This was a heart-warming last evening in Paris.

Next morning, at practically the crack of dawn, Nicole came to take us to the Nord Station. We had entered from the East and had spent four nights and three packed sightseeing days in this great city. Had we exhausted Paris or had Gay Paree exhausted us? Our friendly hotel clerk brightened our day with his fond farewell and parting gifts. Paris had been good to us we decided as we settled back in our train compartment. However, all those millions of people rushing around did make for some uneasiness. It was time to move on to other countries.

We relaxed as our TEE train, the "Parsifal," flashed through the fertile French countryside, cut across eastern Belgium, with its solidly built brick houses, and raced into Germany. The end of a six-hour ride found us by noon in Koln.

A gracious clerk in the railway's gift shop minded our suitcases as we walked out to see the famous Koln Cathedral. This huge Gothic Cathedral, with its two 515 foot towers, is even more striking now than it had been in the past. Strange to say, but this present phenomena has been precipitated by fire bombing during the war which leveled and burnt other buildings in the area. Formerly, the church had been hemmed in on all sides. But, when rebuilding Koln, clear spaces were left purposely so that the Cathedral could stand alone in its impressive tribute to God's glory and the faith of men.

Reclaiming our suitcases, we waited for the airport bus in the underground terminal. We caught an earlier flight for the hour trip to Hamburg, and this gave us an unusual experience. The plane was crowded so we sat on the stewardess' seats and rode backwards! What a sensation on the steep takeoff! Without our seat belts, we would have landed on our faces! This was the first time such a thing had happened and we hope the last time also. Well we couldn't see where we were going, but we could see where we had been as we flew over the flat farming land of Western Germany.

Arriving in Hamburg early did not help us catch an earlier plane to Copenhagen. We still had to wait for Lufthansa OLO at 7:15 p.m. By now we had picked up two nagging worries. One was the news that Heathrow Airport was on strike. With no flights out, how would we be able to go home on the 30th? The other was more immediate. We had no hotel reservations in Copenhagen, so where would we sleep on this night of September 8th?

CHAPTER XIV
CLEAN AIR, HEALTHY APPETITES AND SPARKLING WATERS

Lufthansa treated us royally as we sped through the night to Copenhagen. Every need or desire was satisfied, from food to postcards and stationery, to warm blankets against the cold. There were handsome stewards on this flight and I was thrilled as mine gave me my now treasured Lufthansa lap robe.

All too soon, the Lufthansa bus was transferring us to the SAS Center. We could have stayed in the Scandinavian Hotel here for $100 a night! But we laughed, claiming that much for a bed was just not our style. About $10 a night was. The clerk was very, very nice and helpful. He telephoned various hotels in the city and finally found us accommodations at the Missionshotellet not far from the railroad station. He was a bit worried about our walking the eight or ten blocks to the hotel because the shortest distance was through an unsavory district. Looking neither to the right or left, however, we bravely trundled our cart around the lounging characters in the street. I think they were more astonished at us than we were at them. Our hotel was plain, simple and strict. They even locked the doors at 10 p.m. The next day we discovered we need walk only another half block to a main thoroughfare that passed by the post office. Therefore, we did not take the "shortcut" any more.

We remember Copenhagen as our walking-shopping town. Oh, we did take the "World of Tomorrow" tour to visit the far-advanced social institutions of Denmark. It was a very worthwhile and revealing three hours. We stopped at a day nursery, compared and asked questions; at a low-cost apartment project for older people; at a typical high school, etc. The older people in the Scandinavian countries seem much happier and more secure than the elderly in the rest of the world. The main reason for this is because, after retirement, you have no financial or medical worries. Income tax is high while you are working, but people get a great deal for their money. Doctors are paid by the state, so rural doctors are just as good as those practicing in the city. On our tour bus was a young couple from Newfoundland. They had been bicycling through Denmark when her bike went off the road and she broke her elbow in several places. It took an operation and several specialists to put her arm back together. The couple sadly realized that their vacation would have to be cut short because of the mounting expensive medical treatments. Then to their delighted surprise, the bill was "zero." Denmark has socialized medicine and it covers even accidents happening to foreigners.

Tietgensgade was the street in back of our hotel where the post office was located. Next we traversed the street between the railways and Tivoli. We had much, much walking to do. Down the Besterbrogade, past the Town Radhuspladsen, and into the "Stroget" we went. The "Stroget" is an area of pedestrian streets, packed solid with shops of every description. This is a place where "window shoppers go when they die and have earned heaven." Jewelry, knickknacks, expensive clothes, souvenirs, beautiful glassware, modern furniture, everything is here tempting you to come inside, look, try one, buy. There is only one thing that can keep you from buying. Even we succumbed in our limited way: some beautiful glassware for the convent chapel, warm sweaters for our parents, posters of the year (ducks walking proudly across the main street) for Lorraine's nieces and nephews, and finally heavy stockings and gloves for ourselves as the weather is growing colder each day. (With all the useless stuff we had put into our suitcases, we had never included a pair of shoes. Our Birkenstock sandals had been just fine in the hot weather, but now we were going to use them in snow!)

You can see just about everything in Copenhagen if your legs hold out with all this walking. Down H.C. Andersons Boulevardoss Stormgade and we were crossing to the island where the city was born. Christiansborg Slot (or palace) was the official residence of the kings until 1774. We checked out the Arsenal Museum and the outside of the Stock Exchange building. Then we entered the Holmen Church, which is the royal naval chapel. It was done in complete naval style with the ship motif predominant. The royal guards stood stiff and straight outside the Amalienborg Palace. Next was King Frederick's Church and the museum of Denmark's Resistance Movement. Finally it was good just to stroll through the park and enjoy the Gefion Fountain with its chariot pulled by massive, plunging oxen. Next, the sweetheart of Denmark came into view sitting on her rock. The Little Mermaid is a beautiful and wistful bit of sculpture bringing to life Hans Christian Anderson's story of unselfish love. It was sickening to learn that someone had desecrated the statue by cutting off her head. Fortunately they were able to recast her. So the Little Mermaid still sits there today, sending out her quiet message of tender love.

In the Helligsandskirken there is the most beautiful painting we have ever seen of the Annunciation. It covers the back wall below the pipe organ. Surprised to see this in a Protestant church because they usually do not have such large beautiful paintings.

Only two blocks from our hotel was the famous Tivoli. It was misting the evening we walked through this fairyland with its fountains and shady trees, listening to the music. Color, lights, a world of fantasy, the magic of Tivoli is the stuff dreams are made of, and we were under its spell that night.

Another thing for which the Danes are famous-- in fact we found this to be true also in Norway-- is the quality and quantity of their food. Their hearty breakfast of cold meats, cheese, and fish gave us "going power" to traverse the city, enjoying the sights in the clear air and marveling at the cleanliness of their city.

Only one unpleasant event marred our stay in Copenhagen. We were having lunch in the Central Station Restaurant when a young man stole the purse from an elderly woman. She and her husband were sitting at a table near us and she had put her purse under her chair. Unfortunately, the couple had converted many of their travelers checks into cash in anticipation of moving on in the morning. We tried to be of comfort to them, but actually there was really nothing we or the police could do. It was a lesson to us though to be more careful, for that very week we had come back to our hotel exhausted from shopping and had locked our own purse outside our door!

We met a friend in Copenhagen who was a Holy Names Sister. Sister Mary Katharine had gone back to Denmark to live and now works in a Catholic Information Library. We enjoyed chatting with her as she is a friendly person and told us much about her work there.

We wanted at least a touch of Sweden, so we took the ferry across to Malmo. There we caught the electric train and rode north to the University town of Lund. We always seem attracted to these tree-lined college towns. Need I wonder why! We have visited universities in every country we have visited. While in Lund, we went through the medieval cathedral. It is built of sandstone in Romanesque style and dates back to about 1123. The clock is exceptional. When it plays the hymn "In dulci jubilo," the three Kings emerge to greet the Christ Child.

We walked around the town and Lorraine bought a woolen blue skirt in one of the college shops. Then we rode back through the flat farming landscape to explore Malmo and St. Peter's Church. We returned to Copenhagen on the hydrofoil which type of boat we had never ridden before. Thus excitedly ending our Swedish jaunt.

We left the friendly Danes on Monday and were off to Norway on a SAS late morning flight to Oslo. This is a beautiful city with forests and waterways all within the city limits. This time we knew where we were to stay. Our room at the Norrona Misjonsthatell awaited us. But we couldn't find the hospice. We trundled our cart all around, even up to the Guard House of the Royal Palace where one of the soldiers, wearing his horsetail hat, tried to explain directions in Norwegian. Finally we arrived back at our original starting point and soon found our pleasant hotel only about two blocks away. After putting our gear away, we were off to explore.

The city hall is something very special with its gardens outside and Norwegian art inside.

Tuesday the 13th we devoted entirely to the sights of Oslo. We climbed aboard a sightseeing launch moored at a pier in front of the city hall and operated by an older man and a young girl. We cruised through the islands and along the beaches of the Oslo Fjord. Finally we landed on the Bygdy Peninsula to gaze in wonder at the three Viking ships that have survived for ten centuries. They were used as burial chambers-- one is reputed to belong to Queen Aasa, grandmother of Harold the Fairhaired. Then we examined the Polar Ship "Fram" that took Nansen to the Arctic in 1893 and Roald Amundsen to the South Pole in 1910. Next door was the Kon-Tiki Museum, containing the balsa-wood raft on which Thor Heyerdahl and his companions floated more than 5,000 miles, from Peru to Polynesia, to test the theory that South American Incas may have settled the South Pacific. Then we went by bus to the Norwegian Folk Museum. The open-air section is 35 acres in extent and there are about 170 old buildings. The rural dwellings are grouped together by region of origin, while the urban houses form an "Old Town." The purpose is to show how the people from town and country have lived and worked from the 16th century to the present day. We found all these log buildings and especially the Stave Church most interesting and would have liked to stay longer. But we needed to go out to the countryside over the forested hills to the Holmenkollen, the site of the world's competition ski jumps. The competitions in March are watched by more than 100,000 spectators. The tower is about 165 feet high. I'd hate to ski down that slope! Underneath is a Skiing Museum, tracing the development of the art from a 4,000 year old rock carving via the oldest preserved ski (2,500 years) to present day equipment. This ski jump is so huge that it can be seen for miles.

The Vigeland Sculptures in Frogner Park are just as controversial as the literature said they would be. They depict the life-cycle of man from birth to death and are utterly explicit. Whether they are to your taste or not, everyone has to admit that Gustav Vigeland is a master sculptor.

On the 14th, we caught our train at 10:05 a.m. for our ride across the roof of Norway. We were traveling light, for the hotel was taking care of our heavier baggage. So we relaxed, free as a bird, for our 300 mile ride from Oslo to the seaport of Bergen on the Atlantic Ocean. There are about 200 tunnels on the Oslo-Bergen railway and about 18 miles of snowsheds and 300 bridges. The journey takes about 8 hours. The scenery is varied: green forests, glittering lakes, tumbling waterfalls, narrow valleys, bare and windswept mountain plateaus without so much as a tree. It had snowed the day before we left and the snow lay in drifts on either side of the tracks. Cold! Cold! Cold!

Bergen at last and we made a beeline for the Tourist Center looking for a room. A young man offered to share his with us, but we were not quite that desperate. The accommodation desk found us a lovely room in a private home five blocks up on Vestre Torg Grasse. We bundled up and ventured out into the foggy, rainy night. The good food we consumed warmed and cheered us. Outside the restaurant we followed the sound of music until we found its source. A full band was playing in the park bandstand. A half-dozen spectators under their umbrellas with their backs sheltered by the trees were listening.

We joined them. At the end of a number we would all applaud, the conductor would bow, and then the band would resume. The concert lasted a glorious hour amid falling raindrops. Imagine a whole band playing in that weather just for us! It boggles the mind.

The next morning brought blue skies and mere passing raindrops. We walked all over the town and spent a delightful hour in the Het Aquarium. There we joked and chatted with three young men about the three different possibilities of getting to Flam. We could, of course, take the train back as far as Myrdal and then the Flamshahm down; or take the hydrofoil direct from Bergen to Flam; or ride the train to Voss, transfer to a bus to Gudvangen, then take the ferry to Flam. The young men told us the last option was called "seeing Norway in a nutshell." With their input, we decided upon this third option and hopped on the train in the early afternoon. At Voss, a bus awaited us across from the train tracks. We climbed aboard and the bus headed down the steep hairpin bends of the renowned Stalheim gorge. Besides the passengers, the bus driver delivered mail, packages, and eggs. The views of the mountains were magnificent. Down we went past Stalheim to Gudvangen, where the bus parked at the ferry slip. A boat was seen headed out and a rumor started that we had missed the ferry. After about 15 anxious minutes, a boat was seen far out in the Fjord coming in. It was a huge ferry headed for Vangsnes and Balestrand, both in the opposite direction from Flam. The sailors told us to get on board anyway; and something about walking the plank at midstream? We became a mite uneasy. Strange to say, that is actually what happened. This little hydrofoil from Bergen raced up to the ferry, the sailors shoved a gangplank across, and we looked down into the deep blue waters below. Then we bravely walked across. Once inside the interior cabin of the hydrofoil, we found some tourists from Bergen who had decided on option #2. They informed us that the weather had been foggy and the waves very high and choppy most of the way from Bergen. We were more than ever glad of our decision on option #3. Soon, at the head of the Fjord, a quiet and peaceful little valley awaited us. This was the promised land "Flam." Fearing that it just might storm on the morrow, we immediately caught the last Flam train up and back. This ride was utterly fantastic.

The next day we took the train up and back five times and could have taken it 500 times without tiring of the sights of the wild Flam Valley. Everybody hung out of the back of the train taking pictures. The train then would stop at particularly spectacular scenes and all of us would rush outside until the conductor called us back. Sheer beauty everywhere! Fantastic waterfalls! This 12 mile track, from the Fjord at Flam to Myrdal at the top of the mountain, takes an hour each way. The incline is 55 degrees! And that is the steepest line anywhere!

Our accommodations at the Fretheim Hotel in Flam were perfect. From our window we could look out over the deep blue Fjord to the snow-capped mountains rising up on either side. Our beds were warm and comfortable. The sun was up the next morning before us. How eager we were for our Flambahm rides after our mountain climbing breakfast of eggs, sweet rolls, roast beef, cheese and all the rest of the good food they put on the table.

We would have liked to stay here in Flam for a week of Sundays. But finally it was getting closer to train time, so we took our suitcases with us as we rode up to Myrdal for the last time. There we found our waiting train. Snow was everywhere, dazzling in the bright sunlight. Having an hour before departure to Oslo, we played in the white froth of newly fallen snow. Our Birkenstock sandals with our wool socks worked out quite well. When we got very cold, we shook the snow off our sandals. Then it was back into the pleasant warmth of the waiting train. And we had thought we'd never be cold again after the heat of Israel!

The air here in Norway is so very fresh and clean. This is truly the most beautiful natural country that we have seen. It is hard to believe the scenic beauty outside our train windows. Saw a small town called "Al." Just a pleasant reminder of my dad. We settled back in our seats, enjoying our picnic lunch, as our train rolled back to Oslo and our Norrona Misjonsthotell. It would be great to revisit Norway some day.

CHAPTER XV
WINDMILLS, DIKES, AND BELGIAN HOSPITALITY

The SAS flight from Oslo via Stravanger to Amsterdam on the 17th was very pleasant. We passed over the southern tip of Norway and their naval airfields. Schiphol International Airport was a very busy place, but not so busy that the courteous girl at the tourist desk couldn't find us a room. We picked the Hotel Van Gelder because it had said "bedrooms on the first floor." What they actually meant, we found out, were bedrooms on the first floor above the hotel lobby, which was already up a steep flight of narrow stairs. But as high as we were, the mosquitoes swarmed in. We were fresh meat to them! The red spots on the wall paper were caused by former guests like ourselves swatting the mosquitoes. We added more red blotches to the walls ourselves. Also, this was the only place where we barricaded the outside door at night with our beds. It was a prudent measure.

Usually we rested on Sundays. But Sunday in Amsterdam was filled to the brim and running over. We walked over to St. Nicholas Church near the Central Station for Mass. There we had a very reverent and meaningful liturgy. Afterwards we just walked around the streets. We noted an 11th century church being restored, heard a piano concert, visited Ann Frank's house, and Rembrandt's house. We entered the narrow gateway to the Begiunage, a group of 11th century houses around an inner courtyard. Then we took the tram to the Rijksmuseum and spent hours inside looking at Rembrandt's paintings and his famous "Night Watch." To top off the late afternoon, we ended with a canal trip to see the stately homes bordering the sides of the canals. Some houses had a jutting cross beam with a dangling hook. This was designed so furniture brought by barge could be lifted easily to the upper floors of the homes. Amsterdam, like Venice, is crisscrossed with waterways. But Amsterdam's main ones form ever-winding semicircles around the heart of the town.

Monday morning we took a quick foot tour of "modern" Amsterdam and looked at the shops. Lorraine claims she can absorb the modern culture of the people by these means. Frankly, we are beginning to believe that life is pretty well standardized everywhere.

Off and running again! We took a late morning train to Antwerp, arriving around noon. We had two goals in this modern city: one to see the three Rubens' paintings in the Cathedral of Notre Dame-- Elevation of the Cross, Deposition, and Assumption; and second to visit Rubens' house on 9 Rubensstraat. Mission accomplished, we left for Kortrijk via a slower secondary train.

The train was a bit late, but Francis was waiting for us. A royal welcome and we were off in his car for Ardooie, a small village town. Here we stayed with the Sisters who teach school in the parish. We were given two rooms and an adjoining bathroom. Perfect, no! Ah, but there is a drawback to paradise in Belgium. There is no hot water faucet! And this is true in all the homes, even of those with fancy ornate gold fixtures, as we discovered later in a beautiful modern home that we visited. Either all Belgians are related to the Spartans or there is a secret we haven't discovered as yet!

Every morning after Mass, Francis took us on sight-seeing tours of his native country. Tuesday we visited Brussels and the motherhouse of the CICM Fathers. This has been the heart of the community since their founder started the Society some 110 years ago. They had several thousand pictures of all the Fathers from the time of the founding of the Order until the present day. We amused ourselves trying to find the pictures of the priests we had become acquainted with either in Texas or in Japan. Lorraine found the photo of her friend Fr. William. She had helped him translate his homilies when he first arrived in Texas. But by the end of the second month, he had conquered English and Spanish.

Conversation with these Fathers was very lively. I met Fr. Roger Vandewalle, who had shown my Mom around Hiroshima 25 years ago. He is now stationed in Himeji. Fr. Jennes, who was a former provincial, was also at lunch. Both talked of my Mother, wanted to be remembered to her, and said we looked very much alike. Later on, a Brother took us via the Metro into the center of Brussels. There, at a very fast pace, he practically ran us to the Cathedral, the tomb of the Unknown Soldier, the carillon bells, the headquarters for NATO, and the Common Market, and finally the "Grand Place." This town square is flanked on all four sides by gild-trimmed buildings dating back to the Renaissance. The Guild Halls, like the banks of today, were able to build and richly adorn their business establishments. Then we had to walk down a side street to the Manneken Pis, which has been a tourist attraction for 300 years. At the rate we covered all this territory, I think this Brother must have been a drill sergeant in the Army before he decided to enter a religious community. That evening we enjoyed a quiet dinner with lively discussions

LUCILLE HINTZE

on Belgian political affairs at Francis' brother Paul's home. A welcomed change of pace!

Wednesday, we strolled through the picturesque town of Bruges with its world-famous Belfry, whose carillon weighs 27 tons. We climbed up the tower and inspected the turntable. Lorraine and Francis then continued to climb clear to the top of the 300 foot high structure. Had a super view of this little medieval town, so they said. I had looked at the narrow steep stairs and decided the view from my level was high enough. We leaned over the stone railings of the bridges and looked at the peaceful canals flowing beneath. We examined the art treasures in the Basilica of the Precious Blood and those of St. John's Hospital, where the sick have been taken care of for almost 700 years. We had soup in a little cafe next to the Belfry and were fortified for our next adventure.

We started on our way to Holland along a typical tree-lined Belgian canal until Francis realized we did not have our passports with us. Therefore, he switched to driving along the coast with its flat beaches and sand dunes instead. Then back to Ardooie, straight through the fields of Flanders where the winning of the first World War was aided by the Belgians flooding their land with seawater to bog down the German army. It rained off and on today, but that was no problem since we were in a car. Francis says "typical Belgian weather!"

The historical city of Ghent was our goal in the afternoon where Canon Peter, brother of Francis' sister-in-law, was our guide. He is a professor at the Seminary in Ghent and not only knows the history of the town, but he can also point out in which century each building was erected by the cornices and fringes of the roof. Peter pointed out the problem of "stone cancer" caused by the pollution in the air. More damage is done now in 10 years to the medieval cathedrals than in 1,000 previous years! Tragic! The buildings are not easily repaired because of the high cost.

The highlight of the day was seeing "The Adoration of the Mystic Lamb" by Jan Van Eyck in the Cathedral of St. Bavo. Peter also told us the story of how one of the side pieces was stolen and held for half a million dollars in ransom. The Cathedral officials would not pay the money, so the side painting has never been recovered. It did cost them a quarter of a million though to have the side-piece replaced by a painter. He said they thought that the so-called copy just might well be the original one that was stolen. Such an intriguing mystery! We also viewed "The Conversion of St. Bavo" by Rubens and many other beautiful works of art.

We dashed for our train Friday morning after four perfect days in Belgium. We were both pretty tired as we leaned back in our seats, for not only had Francis shown us all the sights of this land but our evenings were spent visiting his brothers and sisters, plus numerous nieces and nephews. We had talked and talked, and learned much concerning the economic, political and cultural situation of Belgium.

The typical houses here are two-story brick with a large or small farm around them. The houses in the small towns are flush with the sidewalk but have lovely gardens, both flowers and vegetables, in the backyard.

We had one stop to make in Holland before flying to Scotland and that was at Delft. We caught a city bus out to a factory and watched the making and painting of this fine ware. Delft began making its china in the 16th century. One can tell the genuine article by its triple signature: a plump vase topped by a straight line, a stylized letter below it, and the word Delft. We looked over their display of beautiful dishes and tiles until it was time to catch our bus back to the train station. Back we rode to Amsterdam and our flight to Scotland.

CHAPTER XVI
HONEST SCOTSMEN AND CLAN TARTANS

What a plane that took us across the English Channel! It was a small prop job with about 35 passengers and Lorraine could watch the pilot from her seat. The twin engines chugged away into the darkness at barely 300 miles an hour. We thought we might never reach Scotland. But the meal they served would put the larger first-class airlines to shame. Delicious, and so much, that we stored enough nibble food for two whole snacks in our doggie bags. Such service and with one lone stewardess too!

Our arrival in Edinburgh was near midnight and we had no place to lay our heads. However, the young man, who had been seated across the aisle from us, turned out to be "Prince Valiant" in disguise. He knew of and drove us to a very pleasant family "guest home" on Ardmillan Terrace.

Our "guest home" was a quiet and peaceful place. This was very much needed, for we had just learned of Gil's death and burial. Lorraine needed time to struggle with her grief at losing her Dad. For days it rained, both outside and in. Gil was a special person and Scotland was part of his family history he had shared with Lorraine before we had left. In our orginal schedule, we had planned to stay just a day in Scotland. But now because of our present circumstances, we just remained where we were for five days.

Finally, in memory of Gil, we started off on a quest to find the castle, family, tartan, and clan of Dalziel that Gil remembered from his grandparents. We visited several museums, consulted various books and agencies to glean our information. They even sell Clan Maps, we discovered. After finding the very map we wanted, we discovered we didn't have enough money with us to buy it. Forthwith, the elderly street vendor offered to lend us "a pound or two" to tide us over. We were touched at such faith in the honesty of the traveling tourist. Needless to say, we went back to him on the following day to obtain the map. All of the people were friendly here. Also it was good to be back in an English-speaking country where we could be understood easily. We would like to visit the honest Scots again.

Double-decker buses offered us splendid views of all the city sights. We rode down Princes Street in state and noted the contrasting sides. On the north was the bustle and hustle of smart shops and thronging crowds. On the south were green lawns, colorful flowers and an impressive monument which from a distance we thought were the spires of a cathedral. Edinburgh is a good-sized town that still preserves a quiet stateliness.

Of course, we had to go the "Royal Mile" with the Castle at one end and the Palace of Holyroodhouse at the other. Castle Rock is of volcanic origin and is about 443 feet high giving a view of the countryside. The Great Hall houses an interesting collection of weapons and armour. The Scottish Regalia, the Crown, Sceptre, and Sword of State are displayed in a stone-vaulted Crown Room. In 1067, the Saxon Queen Margaret built the beautiful little Norman Chapel in the Castle Citadel. This is Edinburgh's oldest building still in use.

The Royal Mile was for many years the hub of Edinburgh life. The buildings are of stone, very old and well cared for. Some have been homes of nobles; some of merchants. Here also is to be found St. Giles Cathedral and the Parliament House dating from 1639. The Cannongate section is filled with "Kilt Maker and Highland Outfitter" shops. We browsed in and out of these and many more fine Scottish Craft Centers. We discovered the plaid of Gil's clan and bought a scarf in the colors for Lorraine's mom.

Scotland was good for Lorraine in her grief. It brought her closer to Gil by sharing his family heritage with her.

LUCILLE HINTZE

CHAPTER XVII
LONDON TOWN

Wednesday, September 28th, found us flying into London/ Gatwick on British Caledonian. The airport is so far outside the city that it took us an hour by train to get into Victoria Station. The houses here are built solid and squarish, mainly of brick with slate roofs. Found our Bailey's Hotel on Gloucester Road and then a little restaurant for a late lunch around 2 p.m.

We took a bus downtown to Harrods, the largest department store in Europe. It stretches in all directions and dominates the whole shopping area. Being tired and not interested in looking at clothes, I took a chair by the elevator while Lorraine looked at jackets. A half hour went by, and Lorraine had not returned. I became more and more concerned as time wore on and on and on. Still no Lorraine. Finally, after about an hour and a half, she arrived. She had not been able to find which set of elevators was close to me, for there were batteries of them with five different sections selling jackets. All that time gone and still no jacket. Someone was lost, but who?

The next morning we really toured London, gazing at all the buildings. Noted that the church of St. Martin-in-the-Fields should have its name changed. No fields around it now. Marveled at the enormous Houses of Parliament. Then we literally oozed our way through the wall-to-wall people in Westminster Abbey. About the only thing you could see here was the ceiling. There were tiny roped passageways going in different directions and you had to keep your eye on your particular guide's signal-raised umbrella, flag, or whatever, held high. For one minute, they tried for silent prayer. It wasn't to be. So much to see, and impossible to see anything! Another great disappointment was the Changing of the Guard. Too many thousands there also for us to be able to see what was happening. But on our own, we found the London Oratory, which is the second largest Catholic Church in London. The interior of the church is Italian Renaissance style and is extremely beautiful. Not as famous as Westminister Abbey, but a gracious substitute.

We had noticed people queuing for blocks as we rode by in the morning bus. So we decided to join the line when we returned to find out just what the attraction could be. It proved to be the famous Faberge Collection at the Victoria and Albert Museum. Carl Faberge was "Goldsmith to the Imperial Court of Russia." His work "is almost the last expression of court art within the European tradition which brings with it a passionate conviction of the importance of craftsmanship and inventiveness of design, aligned to a celebration of the virtues of wit and fantasy applied to everyday objects, that still has a relevance to the design of today." (Praise by Roy Strong, Museum Director.) And truly, it was remarkable. It is surprising how perfect and how small his pieces are. On the other side of the Museum, we saw a very different type of exhibit. This one was on "Church Change and Decay." Informative, but depressing.

After an early evening meal, we decided to pack. On our last night in a foreign country, we were not going to find ourselves packing at the "midnight hour" as we did at the start of this long trip. After 108 days of travel, we had finally learned our lesson!

As Lorraine brought our clothes in proper order for me to pack, she remarked how they had become worn and were also faded from the blazing sun in Israel. Then last of all, Lorraine handed me our travel guide. As I carefully placed the tattered pages of Arthur Frommer's book "Touring Europe on $5 & $10 a Day" in our suitcase, Lorraine said, "I wish we could thank him some day for helping us make such an interesting, safe, and wonderful trip." "Maybe," I thought, "maybe some day we can." And I stored the idea in my mind.

We decided to break our usual rule and take a cab in the morning to Heathrow Airport. In our wanderings, we had met a cab driver. As he had given us his card, we called him. Harry Burdett of Middlesex was a very honest taxi driver and he charged us only half as much as the hotel clerk claimed would be the price. We were at the airport in plenty of time for our 11:30 a.m. departure. We were there relaxed and with our baggage intact. Ready for takeoff.

LUCILLE HINTZE

CHAPTER XVIII
HOMEWARD BOUND

The TWA plane took off and we were headed home. But as we settled back in our seats, we found that we were just as excited as the day we left San Francisco. But more mature in many ways, we trusted. Yes, we had learned much in the Holy Land. Our sandals had walked over the same ground that Jesus had trod. We had grown in the understanding of Biblical times and the present challenges for Israel. Then the people in Europe, with their customs, culture, all the little things, and the bigger events that happened along the way, helped to change our insights. Oh, there had been some troubling moments on the trip like the stone throwing in Israel, and the Mr. "dark glasses" in Venice.

However, we found that fundamentally all people are friendly and try to be helpful to the bewildered stranger. Our travels have broadened our own outlook on many issues. We are "citizens of the world," we thought, as we passed over the ice fields of Greenland and the tundra of Northern Canada. Within our inner spirits we are so much more than we ever were before. Travel becomes us. It releases us like butterflies from the cocoon.

But now it was 2:40 p.m. on Friday, September 30th, 1977 and we were landing at San Francisco Airport.

LUCILLE HINTZE

OUR ITINERARY

June 13, 1977 Monday San Francisco--New York--Lisbon

June 14--22 Lisbon--Madrid--Granada--Cordoba--Seville--

June 22--23 Barcelona--Rome--Tel Aviv

June 23--July 26 Israel

July 27--30 Tel Aviv--Athens--Rome

August 5--September 8   Train Travel
   Assisi--Firenze--Pisa--Genova--Monte Carlo--
   Avignon--Geneve--Thun--Lucerne--Jungfrau--
   Zurich--Salsburg--Melk--Wein--Murzzuschlag
   Venice--St. Gallen--Basle--Karlsruhe-Stuttgart-
   Mainz--Koblenz--German Rhine Steamer--
   Trier--Paris--Kohn

September 8--30 Flying again
   Kohn--Copenhagen--Oslo--train to Bergen Flam
   Myrdal-back to Oslo--Amsterdam to Brussels--
   Edinburgh--London--San Francisco.

About the Author

After retiring from teaching, Lucille Hintze began her writing career with *Lucille's Harvest* and now continues with *Travel Becomes Us*. This latest book is a memoir of the very first time she and a friend had ever taken a trip outside of the United States. She credits this experiencing of different lands and their cultures as an aid in the understanding of the uniqueness of other nations. Travel, she claims, helps us become more mature citizens of our one global world. Lucille Hintze is a graduate of Stanford University and San Francisco Theological and is a Sister of the Congregation of the Sisters of the Holy Family. She lives in Mission San Jose, California.